TAKE HIM ON A THRILLING EROTIC ADVENTURE. HE'LL WONDER HOW HE EVER LIVED AND LOVED WITHOUT YOU.

For this creative and sensuous guide, Brenda Venus has gathered her exquisite techniques from her own varied erotic experiences and from over a thousand women who have done it all, enjoyed it all, and told it all to Brenda. In frank detail, her new book tells you everything you need to know to find and win your dream lover. She takes you step-by-step, from the first flirtation to that moment when both his desires and your dreams come together. Brenda Venus knows everything about relationships and sex, and she shares it all, including how to

—*keep healthy and beautiful*
—*make an unforgettable first impression*
—*understand the fragile male psyche*
—*make connections and love like never before*

BRENDA VENUS was born in Biloxi, Mississippi. As a very young woman, she met the famous writer Henry Miller and for years maintained a personal relationship with him. In 1986 she published *Dear, Dear Brenda*, a collection of many of the more than 4,000 letters Henry Miller had written to her. She also was close to and corresponded with literary figures Lawrence Durrell and Christopher Isherwood. She has lectured extensively and has had her own radio show. The author of *Secrets of Seduction* (Dutton and Plume), she lives in Beverly Hills.

Brenda Venus

Secrets of Seduction for Women

A PLUME BOOK

PLUME
Published by the Penguin Group
Penguin Books USA Inc., 375 Hudson Street,
New York, New York 10014, U.S.A.
Penguin Books Ltd, 27 Wrights Lane, London W8 5TZ, England
Penguin Books Australia Ltd, Ringwood, Victoria, Australia
Penguin Books Canada Ltd, 10 Alcorn Avenue,
Toronto, Ontario, Canada M4V 3B2
Penguin Books (N.Z.) Ltd, 182–190 Wairau Road,
Auckland 10, New Zealand

Penguin Books Ltd, Registered Offices:
Harmondsworth, Middlesex, England

Published by Plume, an imprint of Dutton Signet,
a division of Penguin Books USA Inc.
Previously published in a Dutton edition.

First Plume Printing, January, 1997
10 9 8 7 6 5 4 3 2 1

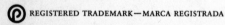

® REGISTERED TRADEMARK—MARCA REGISTRADA

The Library of Congress has catalogued the Dutton edition as follows:
Venus, Brenda.
    Secrets of seduction for women / Brenda Venus.
        p.   cm.
    ISBN 0-525-94103-7 (hc.)
    ISBN 0-452-27794-9 (pbk.)
    1. Sex instruction for women.   2. Women—Sexual behavior.
    3. Sexual excitement.   4. Man-woman relationships.   I. Title.
HQ46.V45   1996
613.9'6'082—dc20   95–20548
                                                                  CIP
Printed in the United States of America
Original hardcover design by Julian Hamer

To all women—

Your life is similar to a song. Not only do you compose, arrange, and play it; you sing it as well. You instinctively choose the tone and the key. And the man you love should complement your melody with his harmony. But each man will have his own special voice—no two men are the same. And when you meet your soul mate, your song will carry his name . . .

—BV

Acknowledgments

From my heart I thank:

My magnificent editor, Ed Stackler, for giving shape and perspective to the material and for being sensitive to my artistic needs. My wonderful agent, Alan Nevins, for always finding a good home for my books. My heart's blood, choreographer Yuri Smaltzoff, who keeps my life moving in a positive direction. Poet Clive Brewster, who inspired me to reach higher goals. Rocket scientist Dan Bloxsom, for donating generously of his time throughout the final stages of production. Attorney Mark Ukra, for his legal expertise and invaluable support. My personal physician, Dr. Harvey Cantor, who not only kept me physically alive but also apprised me of all the newest medical advances. Patty Formeca, who on short notice dropped everything to further and enhance my work. And Dr. John Minoli, who, in spite of being on call around the clock, always found time to contribute his invaluable insights and endearing humor.

And finally, all the warm and beautiful souls who contributed their private thoughts and expertise and lent me a shoulder.

Contents

4—Acts of Love

5—If Things Go Wrong: Troubleshooting

Introduction

Love looks not with the eyes, but with the mind,
And therefore is winged Cupid painted blind.
—SHAKESPEARE

Do you want to know what men are dying to tell you about their secrets, their innermost passions, but can't?

I have been in love with the "brotherhood of the sperm" ever since I became conscious of them at age six. I had some starry-eyed notion that they were like us, except for their large outer organ, of course. They are not. And yet . . .

Years later, after experiencing great love and even greater pain, and growing from those experiences, I wanted to understand more about men deep inside their souls—their very thoughts and dreams. So I got busy—studying, traveling, investigating, and interviewing over one thousand men of diverse age, race, and wealth from around the world.

Of course, it wasn't easy getting to the core of men's emotional sensibilities, but it was rewarding. And I will share with you this rich and hard-won knowledge of men's needs, wants, and sexual desires. To really understand your man—to understand what he wants in a woman—you have to breathe him, taste him, and get inside his blood. Therein lies the reason for this book.

At times, gathering information was like stealing their most guarded secrets; underneath their brazen veneer, many men were actually shy, socially reticent, and full of mistrust. But once comfortable and relaxed, they courageously poured forth their true feelings and insights. My heart was touched many times while hearing some very moving and intimate revelations. And, yes, I gained a new respect for the men with whom we share our planet.

Consequently, my goal is to offer you the tools to understand your man's inner thoughts and feelings, interpret his masculine behavior, peel away his protective armor and reach into his soul, thereby becoming a magnificent, loving seductress.

In the process, you will also discover a man's turnons and turnoffs, his likes and dislikes. I'll teach you how to cope with rejection by turning negatives into positives and . . . how to choose the *right* man while staying away from the *wrong* man.

It all begins with us females. Ever since the day Eve enticed Adam to bite the apple, *you* have been choosing the time, the place, and the man with whom you wish to interact. You have the power to say either yes or no—to accept or reject. So take an honest look at yourself and decide what you really want. Learn exactly what you can and cannot live with in a man.

Never forget: you are a woman. You are a goddess. You are in control. Make your move! If you want a good man, picture him in your mind and nurture the same qualities you wish to attract. Self-awareness, self-improvement, and self-esteem are your keys. Remember, you must first become that which you hope to find. It's not about a season, fashion, or fad. It's about *real love*!

Chapter 1

What Makes a Seductress

WHAT MAKES A SEDUCTRESS

*Someone who does not run
toward the allure of love
walks a road where nothing lives.*
—RUMI

You can be a magnificent seductress. At this very moment you may already be one in someone else's eyes whether you know it or not. Do you find that hard to believe? You must have had some hope that it could be true or you wouldn't be reading this book. So take a deep breath and relax . . . your hope led you to the right place, a place where the seductive arts *can* be learned and the secrets are revealed with every page you turn.

Many women don't think of themselves as seductresses because their understanding of seductiveness is too narrow. They think of Marilyn with her gorgeous body and raw sexuality combined with her vulnerable fragility. Or they think of Cher with her terrific figure, outrageous clothes, and intrepid attitude. Then they look in the mirror and if they don't look like Marilyn or Cher (and, after all, very few of us do), they decide that they're not seductress material. What utter nonsense!

Seductresses come in all shapes, sizes, and ages. Was Marilyn a seductress? You bet! Is Cher? Absolutely! Their sexual energy and magnetism could never be mistaken or overlooked. But in a different way, Grace Kelly was also a seductress. Men sensed (correctly) that her cool exterior concealed a volcanic na-

4 • BRENDA VENUS

ture. Audrey Hepburn? Oh, yes. Her charm and vitality drew men and women to her. Ingrid Bergman? Her freshness made men long to be loved by a woman like her. No one who saw *Casablanca* had any problem believing that Humphrey Bogart and Paul Henreid both wanted her.

Garbo's air of mystery made men dream. Dietrich with her suggestion of the dominatrix made them thrill. Michelle Pfeiffer, slinking on a piano in *The Fabulous Baker Boys* or cutting a swath through old New York in *The Age of Innocence*, is a lesson in seductiveness. Meg Ryan, with her exuberance, made us glad that Tom Hanks finally found her at the end of *Sleepless in Seattle*. Lena Horne becomes more bewitching with every passing decade. And it's more than mere beauty that makes Julia Roberts light up the screen.

In fact, being a seductress has very little to do with beauty but everything to do with a confident attitude, energy, humor, charm, playfulness, genuineness, sensuality, and *knowing*. These qualities turn men on.

Most of the men I interviewed envision their dream girl as follows: she is sensitive to my needs. She is spontaneous. She loves to make love. I feel all of her focus is on me. She seems to sense when to be aggressive and when to submit. She's not afraid of her womanhood or her vulnerability. She never fails to compliment the way I please her. She's vocal about her pleasure, and she is quick to guide me in pleasing her. She's always different, never predictable, never indifferent. She suggests role playing. She's always inventive, fun, exciting, and willing to try something new. She's like Sheena of the Jungle one minute, delicate and demure the next. She doesn't mind if I watch while she turns herself on. She's not ashamed of her body even when she feels overweight. She knows exactly what turns me on and what doesn't. She talks sexy to me on the phone. She teases me in restaurants and driving home in the car. She lets me know when she wants to make love in a seductive and feminine way. If I'm tired, she doesn't pout and make me feel guilty. And when she's not in the mood, she's very gentle and sensitive to my feelings. She makes me feel like a combination of Don Juan, Casanova, and Rudolph Valentino. She knows what to do when I'm feeling down. She understands when I need silence. She makes sounds during lovemaking, and she expresses her fantasies. She's full of surprises—the kind I like. She's smart but not so much that she intimidates me, just enough to arouse thought. But *most important*, she touches my heart, and that's a mystery I can't explain.

To be a skillful seductress, you need to find out your man's likes and dislikes—what excites, hurts, tickles, or makes him uncomfortable. Just as you may want your clitoris stroked through your panties, he may want his testicles held and properly squeezed. Maybe that makes him feel terrific. Then again, maybe he hates it. You need to explore his body gently. Does he respond to a lot of pressure or a little? When stroking, does he prefer light or firm, long or short, or both? Does he want you to use both hands together or one hand on his shaft with the other hand on his scrotum? Does he like slurping sounds, hummms and ahhhs, or no sound at all? Does he like it when you talk to his penis, or does it make him feel silly? Watch his facial expressions, listen to his moans and groans, and pay close attention to the way his hands move your hands.

What does he like when he's really hot, and what does he enjoy when he's not? Do you know how to make him more aroused? Do you know how to cool him down? His mind and body are in the power of your magic hands, your magic mouth and tongue—your magic spell.

Learn to vary your rhythms and draw the utmost

pleasure from his body. Watch how he touches, strokes, and plays with himself, if he's not shy. Be sensual and passionate with both yourself and him. Give him lots of love and understanding, and don't force him to perform. It isn't the circus. He's only a man. Most men have plenty of secret desires that they may find difficult to express. Give him time and space. Be patient. Eventually, he will trust you enough to expose all of himself to you.

It's best to keep a little something in reserve for a special evening. Every day is not the Fourth of July, nor should it be. The Fourth of July is a spectacular display of fireworks exploding and floating through the night sky accompanied by the rousing music of a Sousa march. Magnificent! But every night? Some nights you might prefer the quiet beauty of moonlight reflected on the water, while listening to soft strains of a violin.

Don't give everything you've got all at once. Remember—the art of seduction is the science of restraint!

Always please yourself first and never, ever do anything that makes you feel uncomfortable. Whatever you do, do it with your whole heart, body, and soul, and you will find yourself greatly loved in return.

HOW TO BE A SEDUCTRESS

Pursuit and seduction are the essence of sexuality. It's a part of the sizzle.

—CAMILLE PAGLIA

- Genuine confidence begins with knowing your own body and mind.
- Knowledge is your ultimate love power.

- Develop good communication skills both in and out of the bedroom.
- Listen more than you speak, unless talk is related to both of you. Your conversation should always be positive and sensual.
- Be relaxed and self-assured.
- Know exactly what you're doing and why. Learn your man's mind, emotions, body, and sex organs.
- Appeal to all his senses: touch, taste, smell, sight, and sound.
- Find the right lighting for the mood you want to set.
- Create a romantic atmosphere. Arrange furniture to suit your sexual expression.
- Make him feel comfortable and relaxed in your environment. Welcome him with his favorite beverages, snacks, and music.
- Show enthusiasm when he speaks; have a twinkle in your eye. Flirt.
- Value cleanliness. Both you and your man should be able to lick, suck, probe, rub, squeeze, massage every square inch of one another without hygienic concerns or inhibitions.
- Go slow with all thoughts and actions. Be gentle and tender. Savor every moment. Tease.
- Kiss your man as though it were the first time, every time. Imagine that your lips are your nether lips and your mouth is your clitoris and his lips are the tip of his penis and his tongue is the shaft. That will be a kiss to remember!
- Learn the art of massage—of both body and mind.
- Listen to his body language and sounds. He will tell you all you need to know, even if silently.
- Do what pleases you both.

- Explore. Be adventurous. Find the things that really turn him on. If he doesn't like something you're doing, move on. If he does, stay with it.
- Don't be afraid to experiment.
- Relish every part of his body as though it were your "last supper."
- Create your own fantasies and then *live* them.

WHEN MEN WANT IT

Sex is impersonal, and may or may not be identified with love. Sex can strengthen and deepen love . . .
—HENRY MILLER, *The World of Sex*

Men are *always* ready to love and be loved, and that *sometimes* may translate into sex. For example, when men come home to relax from a hard day at work . . . they want it. After they fulfill their daily obligations and chores . . . they want it. Even while walking down the street . . . they *want it*! The bottom line: the penis is crying out for love—touch me, kiss me, suck me, fondle me, stroke me, take my gondola down your warm, wet canal—anything . . . just pay *attention* to me, woman!

And if there is no one around to fill his dance card, he just might have to take matters into his own hands. Marlon Brando said of playing Stanley Kowalski in *A Streetcar Named Desire*, "I think Stanley was like me —very physical. And I think that Stanley would have liked to put his hands in his pockets and feel himself." Marlon is putting his finger on the fact that most men are driven by a common and mischievous motivator: namely—testosterone. The sheer enthusiasm of watching his penis rise from a snooze is part of man's identity; and, in large part, it is what guides and rules a man's thinking and behavior.

A man's "glands" stand especially at attention on weekends—Friday night, Saturday morning, Saturday night, Sunday morning. Vacations are also a fabulous time for sex. It's playtime! After exercising and sweating at the gym, a man walks away feeling particularly good about himself . . . and Willie wants sex. After watching a provocative movie, reading a titillating story, or talking to his girlfriend over the phone, he wants sex. If he could, he might actually climb through the phone!

A man wants sex in different ways, too, based on his mood. Sometimes he wants wild, steamy sex; sometimes he wants gentle, soft, and romantic sex; sometimes he wants role-playing. One of the more popular fantasies revolves around aggressive, dominating women. (You play the teacher, he plays the student; you play the goddess, he plays your slave; you play the doctor, he plays the patient; you play the figure skater, he plays the fan; you play the Playmate, he plays the photographer.)

A lot of times, a man would like to do something about the yens of his penis but it's neither the right time nor the right place. That in itself can be very erotic. At such moments, he remains civil, cultivated, and controlled. But deep in his thoughts, even while reviewing statistics or going over the numbers, there are subliminal longings simmering.

Some men carry out their fantasies to such a degree that these dreams become part of their lifestyle. One such couple with whom I spoke are Margo and Sam. They are a respectable couple; they live by outward appearances. But they carry on a wild fantasy life behind closed doors. She plays mistress to his submissive tendencies and reduces him to the role of sex toy—his only purpose in life is to please her. He does the housework, cooks meals, and at her whim drops to his knees to serve her with his silver tongue and his golden organ.

On a typical evening, Sam arrives home from work clad in his proper business suit. He immediately changes into his black jumpsuit and nail-studded leather collar. Margo, meanwhile, dons her thigh-high black leather boots, straps on her corset and garter belt, and sits down to watch TV. She likes scotch and soda and little cigars, which Sam provides at the snap of her fingers. Sam then sits in the corner of the room, waiting for her orders.

On any given night, Margo lets Sam stroke himself while she masturbates. But on special nights, when she, of course, is in the mood, she directs him to explode quickly. Sometimes, she lies down, parts her legs, and orders Sam to kneel between them. If she feels Sam has been good, she lets him part her lips with his tongue. After a long while, she orders him deeper inside. After these sessions, Sam falls back and fixes Margo a nightcap.

Ladies, you don't have to work as hard as Margo to get the same results. Why don't you start by whispering your fantasies in your lover's ears between kissing and nibbling on them. He would love hearing a story (note: story!) from you of domination, or of him joining you with another woman, or any lascivious picture that pops into your pretty head. Remember: you don't care where he gets his appetite, as long as he eats at home.

CONFIDENCE

To love oneself is the beginning of a lifelong romance.
—OSCAR WILDE

Although youth's for an hour and beauty's a flower, confidence will win you the world. Confidence is an aphrodisiac. When you have it, everybody wants a taste. That is the very reason that nothing is more sexually appealing to a man than a confident woman.

Have you ever been at a party or social affair and wondered what a certain woman surrounded by a bevy of interesting and attractive men had that you didn't? Confidence! It makes up for any lack of physical endowment.

You're not born with confidence. You acquire it. It's a learned skill. Granted, some people come by it naturally, but that's uncommon. More often, arrogance, snobbery, or plain pushiness masquerade as confidence, and in time people discover the ruse. But anyone can gain confidence if the desire to learn is genuine. Be determined. Learn to love yourself by readjusting your mind-set.

It requires practice but presents pitfalls because many of you have been taught, either deliberately or unconsciously, *not* to love yourself. *Now* is the time to relearn. Whether you were raised by loving, caring parents, dysfunctional parents, or no parents, the choice is yours. Practice making the correct choices so that they become as habitual as brushing your teeth. Then you'll be on your way to making it a way of life.

I've talked to women who were raised in a storybook family and grew up with low self-esteem. On the other hand, I've talked with women who were raised by abusive, insensitive parents, yet have acquired self-respect and success because they disciplined themselves. Let's explore some ways to build, maintain, and reinforce your self-respect.

1. Set high but reachable goals.
2. Work hard and complete one goal before moving on to the next one. Finishing a task or goal,

however menial (such as waxing your floors),
produces a sense of accomplishment.
3. Appreciate and reward yourself for a job well
done.
4. Cultivate friends who appreciate you. Develop
your own support group.

Conversely, fear and lack of self-respect are very
destructive enemies. A man comes to a woman for reassurance and a shoulder on which to lean—someone
to tell him he's okay. If you appear confused and afraid,
you'll have no power to reassure him and he will probably go to a woman who feels secure and can do the
job.

If you find yourself in a tragic situation and it's
tough to face the day, read this poem. Then pick yourself up and get busy. I keep it on my refrigerator door
as a constant encouraging reminder. It helps immensely.

Don't Quit

When things go wrong as they sometimes will,
When the road you're trudging seems all uphill,
When the funds are low and the debts are high
And you want to smile, but you have to sigh,
When care is pressing you down a bit,
Rest, if you must, but don't you quit.

Success is failure turned inside out—
The silver tint of the clouds of doubt,
And you never can tell how close you are,
It may be near when it seems so far;
So stick to the fight when you're hardest hit—
It's when things seem worst that you must not quit.

—Unknown

Remember: a winner never quits, and a quitter never wins.

The first step on your road to success is having a *positive attitude*. Your attitude toward life, yourself, and men in general, can lead to success or failure. Everyone has imperfections and bad days, but you can be a compelling person as long as you don't make a big deal out of your shortcomings. And please, ladies, when you're on a date with a man, don't tell him about your cellulite and excess weight. He does not care. What he does care about is that you're comfortable with yourself, flaws and all. A little cellulite, a few extra pounds, and a tiny bump on your nose are not the end of the world.

A man asks a woman for a date because he obviously likes what he sees. Mark, a thirty-eight-year-old tennis pro said, "I hate going out with a drop-dead beautiful woman who poses, acts uncomfortable with herself, and always looks around the room. I'd rather date a confident woman with a good sense of humor. If she likes herself, I know I'm in for a good time."

Know exactly what you want and go after it with all your might. Be specific. Visualize your goal as though you already have it. That means you can imagine what you want and *will* it to happen. The power of the mind is very potent indeed. Take your time and see every detail in your head—imaginatively feel it, smell it, touch it. But be realistic. Don't visualize yourself married to the desirable John Kennedy, Jr., or some famous man you're not likely to meet. (If you get a chance to meet him, however, go for it! Now that you've worked on your confidence and self-respect, you deserve him!) If you're determined and believe in yourself, nothing will stop you because you know exactly what you want, where you're going, and why. *Whew!* Big exercise for the ol' brain, but it works.

Be pro-active—take more interest in the world around you. Join groups. It doesn't cost much to know more. Take classes. Learn to paint, play music, dance, read faster, write, speak another language, decorate, garden, cook, fix cars . . . whatever you desire. When you become an interesting person, full of knowledge and exciting ideas, interesting, desirable men will be seeking you out.

Get rid of misdirected, shotgun criticism and negativity. They're your enemies. With practice, your mind can switch to positive thoughts at will instead of sloshing around in negative ones. In fact, it usually takes less effort. Cleanse yourself of that negative inner voice telling you that you're unworthy, useless, stupid, ugly, fat, et cetera. Say to yourself, "Gorgeous is as gorgeous does!"

In the event you get stuck on a negative, read something funny or uplifting. Call a witty, positive friend. (You can't cultivate too many of these!) Play some upbeat music and dance around the room. Take a walk around the block, breathe the fresh air, and smell a flower. Exercise. Go see a funny movie. Wash the windows, scrub the floors. Make yourself busy doing whatever works for you. But erase all negativity from your mind and replenish it with good, healthy, clean thoughts. (Good, healthy, dirty thoughts work, too!)

Never judge yourself by how you look in a miniskirt or whether you think men find you attractive. You don't need a man to tell you that you're beautiful. Know your assets and work hard to make them even better. Okay, so you don't look like the latest supermodel, film, or soap star. It's not important. You have your own uniqueness, your own great qualities. Cultivate an appreciation for who you are. Don't be your own pit bull. Replace *"attack, attack, attack"* with *"advance, advance, advance."*

You're living and breathing *now*, so create with the clay that God gave you, and mold yourself into a goddess. Be thankful that you have something to work with—great hair, great legs, great buttocks, great hands and feet, or whatever. And if you don't have 'em, build 'em, shape 'em, tone 'em, any way you want 'em. Have a romance with yourself. Think and feel that you're the best or that you can be the best. Then make yourself the *best*.

Take a few hours a week just for yourself. Pampering doesn't cost a lot of money. Draw up a bubble bath. Have a glass of champagne or wine. Light some incense and candles. Turn on your favorite music and surrender to the seduction of warm water and bubbles. Also, paint your toenails red, get a friend to massage your back and shoulders. Lie in the sun for fifteen minutes. A little vitamin D and sunshine will do wonders for your soul. Exercise and sweat all those toxins out of your system. I guarantee, you'll feel like the person you're supposed to be. Maybe ripe, juicy, red strawberries are in season, but you think they're too expensive. What's a little extravagance once in a blue moon? Enjoy a few of life's graces from time to time, and in the process *learn* to enjoy life in the here and now.

I like to use a character that I've named "Betty Can-Do" as an example: She's the epitome of a confident woman. No one can emulate Betty's confidence, because she reinvents herself as she goes along. Her presence, her aura, her magnetism can be mystifying to people. She climbs the ladder quickly, gets the man she wants, and has other women vying for her attention. Betty writes the book instead of following what's in it. She's a pioneer and a heroine in her own right. She's positive, she's curious, she's a motivator, she's a perpetual student, and she's honest with herself and her

fellowman. Betty doesn't have to trick, pretend, or ca-
jole, because she believes in herself and her accomplishments. She's creative and spontaneous in lovemaking.
She's not afraid to surrender to her man or her orgasm,
because she wants the best. What she doesn't know, she
learns. The magic that surrounds Betty arouses loyalty
and enthusiasm, and her appeal always finds her at the
center of attention. So why not create your own favorite
character. There's no reason why you can't do what
Betty Can-Do!

BODY TALK

*The academy has fought stoically to claim that they
named the Oscar. But of course I did. I named it after
the rear end of my husband!*

—BETTE DAVIS

Your body is perpetually dancing. It dances to the silent
sounds of your hands, heart, eyes, face, smile—and the
rest of your body parts. It may not chime in tune, but
you can be sure it's talking. It's show-me rather than
tell-me time. Even while making love, your body dances
with your beloved. Usually, he leads; sometimes you
lead. In love's embrace, organic rhythms are essential.

Now consider that most communication is nonverbal. At least two-thirds of the time you communicate
without words. Clearly, your body language should be
honed to convey subtle needs. After all, the language of
the body is a fine art and should be viewed as such. The
adept are never misunderstood in their communication.
Their intoxicating mind-body cocktail is communicated
to the high octane, the highbrow, and the in between.
Whereas the inept are always misunderstood, unclari-
fied, and unfinished—always strung out. Be aware that

your slightest movement is sending signals. Stay honest with your body-brain communication, and you're sure to find a relationship anchored in romanticism and respect.

For those of you who are bogged down in domesticity at home with nigh a farthing of sexual interest in your husband's eyes, you need to rekindle the spark and become that hot tamale he fell in love with many moons ago. But before you try to turn him on begin by turning yourself on. A turned-on woman is an exciting woman. Start by practicing an array of provocative poses in front of a mirror.

Marilyn Monroe used to do it. She would paint her lips with layers of lipstick and shiny gloss, then practice different ways of speaking while making her lips as sensual as possible. She cracked herself up before she turned herself on. Her lips were sending a silent, erotic message. She also practiced wiggling her derriere seductively enough to turn the mirror on! No wonder all those cameramen were falling over one another to snap a shot or catch a glimpse in between. All the effort certainly worked for Marilyn—why not you?

For scintillating ideas, thumb through an issue of *Playboy*, *Penthouse*, or other inspirational magazines and imitate how the girls position their faces, their bodies, their eyes—note what they're doing with their hands, fingers, lips, tongue, legs, derriere, breasts, and feet. In other words, see how their total being is talking. Notice how the suds from their bath sensually fall off their nipples or clitoris. Observe what they're wearing —jewelry, shoes, teddies, lingerie, street clothes, wet see-through blouses, shirts, and skirts. Which hairstyles and cosmetics are exciting to you? Try it! But take only the ideas that work for your particular body and attitude.

Did you know that centuries ago, long before the

advent of glossy magazines, women were using classical statues, portraits on canvas, or whatever the means of that time, as models to imitate sensual stances? They were posing seductively even then. Posing like the magazine models can get you started, but once you get into the mood and turn yourself on with your own inventiveness, I'm sure your man won't be able to unzip his trousers fast enough.

If you feel stupid and ridiculous strutting and posing, I suggest you do what feels natural to you. Maybe when you're dressing, bend over slightly while buckling your shoe and hold the position until you know he notices the unforbidden. Put your stockings on slowly so he can look at your beautiful legs being dressed in silk. Or put a string of pearls around your neck and a pair of high heels on your feet, then sit naked in front of your mirror, legs slightly parted while fixing your makeup and hair. Do what you do best, only do it in front of him. A word to the wise: don't do your sexual strutting while he's in the middle of an important sports event on television, or he'll have one eye on you and the other on the game.

Once, when I was guesting on a talk show, a very lovely lady was advocating that people make their time for sex by marking it on their calendars. That might be practicable for some, but I work twelve hours a day, and if I had to circle a day on my calendar for a sexual rendezvous with my man, I would feel silly. There's no need to mark your calendar for sex when you can turn whatever moment you choose into an erotic event with just your body language. Send loving nonverbal messages to him every day in one endearing way or another.

BODY BEAUTIFUL

To be born woman is to know—
Although they do not speak of it at school—
Women must labour to be beautiful.

—W. B. YEATS

You are what you truly believe you are! Begin with an honest evaluation of yourself by standing totally naked in front of a mirror. Don't be cruel, rather be constructive about areas you want to improve. Squint your eyes and imagine your fantasy shape. Looks good, huh? Feel proud and confident, because you want to remember *that* feeling. Your goal . . . creating "body beautiful," by you!

The human body is a magical instrument. It's breathtaking in its intricacy and, when well tuned, operates in a predictable manner which will respond to your commands. For example, imagine your body as a piece of clay and your mind as a tool. Direct it to eat only certain foods; direct it to exercise three times a week for at least thirty minutes; direct it to think positive thoughts; direct it to read, study, and learn. It will culminate in a beautiful, well-balanced shape—substantial from the inside and out. The power is yours. Claim it and make it your own!

Would you like to take off a few pounds and tone up? Almost everyone I know would like to lose a few. But just dropping weight is not the issue. Making yourself excited enough to create a better you is the issue. You can motivate yourself with proper focus, hard work, and discipline. That's the secret to success—and the path toward your lifelong goal of "body beautiful." See it, hold that vision, then become it. Leave notes and pictures around your home and workplace for encouragement. I have a poster of a terrific body with no face in my gym. Believe me, it works, especially when I feel lazy.

Have you ever noticed that the people you think are so beautiful are not really that beautiful if you look closely at their features? They are beautiful to you because they look healthy. Their hair and eyes shine. Their skin glows. Their cheeks and lips are rosy. They have confidence. And they have a wonderful smile—a magnetic smile. Healthy-looking people are like magnets. Everybody wants to be around them.

Health is *everything*. If you want to reap the benefits of a healthy body and a healthy mind, you need to sow the finest seeds. Eat well, sweat (which means putting yourself on an exercise program), and sleep. Get lots of sleep. If possible, get in a good eight hours a night, plus a fifteen-to-twenty-minute nap, appropriately called "beauty rest." I realize for most of you, this is an adaptive challenge, but it's worth striving for.

Finally . . . to complete the picture of a totally beautiful you, you need to nourish your mind—read, read, read with some sense of purpose. Educate yourself: get familiar with current events. Investigate. Listen to the news. Buy magazines that enlighten you. Take a class that you're interested in at a nearby adult school so you'll develop and have your own opinions. Every woman needs to have opinions that she genuinely feels, thinks, and believes.

A good man will respect your point of view even if he doesn't agree with it. He will support who you are and what you want to do in life. The wrong man will put you down at every turn, hold you back from attaining your goals, make you feel foolish for no reason, and stifle your creativity. If he doesn't get with the program . . . walk away.

EATING RIGHT

One of the best weight-loss exercises consists of placing both hands against the table edge and pushing away. That's definitely a secret to fitting into your clothes. But the greatest secret is: "You are what you eat." Period. True beauty is a by-product of good health. To look your best, you must eat nutritious foods.

Stop dieting! What a depressing word. To a woman, the word *diet* carries the same connotation as the word *commitment* to a man. Don't use the word, don't even think about it. Most fad diets are a waste of time and energy. And they serve to reinforce negative feelings. Instead, put yourself on a "program" of eating in a balanced way and exercising. But don't allow your world to revolve around food. That's not living. That's existing. Eat to live, don't live to eat. That's not who you are. You're not a hamburger and fries, cookies, or a quart of ice cream. You're a beautiful person with a lot to offer the world. Let's get on with the "eating right" program. The following is my basic eating pattern for breakfast, lunch, and dinner. It's filling, it's nutritious, it fuels my body and mind. The portions are always small but sturdy.

BREAKFAST

After awakening, I drink one or two eight-ounce glasses of water, walk around, read the paper, and generally get my body functioning before I begin work. Then I grind Vienna roast coffee beans and brew one cup of coffee (sometimes I have tea), adding half-and-half. If you like cream in your coffee and need to watch your calories, it's best to use low- or nonfat milk. Never drink coffee in abundance. A cup a day is OK—five is not. I avoid refined sugar and don't care for the taste of saccharin, so I use honey whenever I want something sweetened.

Almost every morning, I eat steel-cut oats (it's a heartier, more nutritious kind) with thin slices of either banana, papaya, apple, peach, or strawberries on top. When I get bored with oatmeal, I alternate with either one whole egg and one egg white, four egg whites scrambled, or an omelette with egg whites and spinach, and a piece of wheat toast—sometimes plain, sometimes with jam or honey. I drink freshly squeezed orange juice when I'm not too lazy to squeeze.

After I eat anything, I brush and floss my teeth. Then I'm less inclined to want anything sweet. It's a good habit for you, too! Try it!

And I also take vitamin and mineral supplements with my meals for better assimilation.

LUNCH

I teach ballet several mornings a week. On those days, I eat a heftier lunch consisting of baked or roasted chicken, or white tuna fish in water, accompanied by a green vegetable, carrots, and half a baked yam. On the other days, I eat sliced turkey and a fresh vegetable salad. When I'm writing a new book, I become so involved that I might just eat plain yogurt and fruit, or angel-hair pasta with sliced tomatoes, virgin olive oil, and lemon juice. When I'm in a work mode, I don't eat because I'm hungry; I eat because my brain needs the nutrition in order to concentrate and create. I feel nervous and tired without nutritious food.

"An apple a day keeps the doctor away" is the best advice I could give you for maintaining a regular digestive system. Also a few prunes a day are internally beneficial. These healthy items can be interspersed as a light snack to quell the midday appetite.

DINNER

I usually eat light in the evening—a spinach salad with hard-boiled egg whites and maybe white fish, shrimp, or salmon; or maybe plain yogurt with fresh fruit. Or, if I'm really tired, I'll have a bowl of wheat-grain cereal with raisins. And in summer, sometimes I just eat a huge slice of watermelon. Although it is most difficult, I try not to eat after seven o'clock in the evening.

ALCOHOL

One or two times a week, I drink a glass of wine or champagne. But I have gone for months without any alcoholic beverage while working long, grueling hours. During this time, I'm on a stringent schedule. Like a warrior—everything I eat, everything I do must feed my creative mind. I can't allow anything to slow my creative process, and even a glass of wine can make me sluggish the next morning. There is plenty of time to celebrate when I've finished the project.

Since too much alcohol can dry the skin and cause weight gain, you should be careful with your intake. If you must drink, a wine spritzer is refreshing and lower in calories.

The taste of a good wine or champagne is most welcome. One or two glasses now and then is both pleasurable and relaxing. My favorite champagne is Taittinger Rosé, but it's a luxury that my pocketbook frowns upon. However, on special occasions (my birthday, Christmas, or upon completing a project that I've slaved over for months), I buy a bottle and share it with good friends.

MEAT

Rarely do I eat red meat or organs, although liver and onions or a filet mignon gives me needed energy when I'm sluggish. For a real treat, I drive to the Apple Pan, a home-style diner, where I sit at the counter and order one of their delicious hamburgers with fries and a root beer. It makes me feel like I'm in high school again and adds to the emotional charge of the outing. But eating hamburgers is an *exception*. That's why it's a treat. Häagen-Dazs ice cream is another of my favorite treats. But a treat is a treat—a reward for something well done or a boost for a melancholic mood.

SWEETS

On candy, desserts, and snacks: Yes, I do eat a chocolate now and then (white chocolate is one of my passions). When I'm at a restaurant, I sometimes order lemon or fruit desserts—apple, berries, peaches, or whatever fruit is in season. I don't crave snacks because I drink eight to ten glasses of water a day. Water will cut down your appetite and you won't be as inclined to snack. Depending on the person and the climatic conditions, our bodies are composed of 94 percent to 97 percent water by weight. So it makes good sense to drink plenty of it, preferably bottled or tap free from contamination. If you must snack, dried fruits or freshly cut fruits and vegetables—carrots, cucumbers, apples— are a healthy choice.

SUPPLEMENTS

Vitamins and minerals are terribly misunderstood. They can be harmful when taken in excessive amounts or on an empty stomach. No one can tell you precisely how much to take because individual absorption rates vary widely. For best results, consult a nutritionist.

Remember that the human body cannot live on vitamins alone; it also needs good nutritious food to survive. Vitamins can never substitute for fresh food. Too many people make the mistake of trying to live on a severe diet of lettuce, water, and fifty vitamins. Your tendons, bones, and muscles will suffer.

I take a multitude of vitamins from time to time, but it's usually when I'm pumping iron, teaching, traveling, and working harder than I should. However, I always eat a variety of healthy foods with the addition of vitamins A, B complex, C, D, and E, calcium, iron, magnesium, and zinc. Magnesium is helpful for restless sleep, and the mineral chromium picolinate can cut down your craving for sugar and stimulate the activity of enzymes. I also pay heed to the fact that excessive alcohol, smoke, and caffeine contribute to bone loss in women.

The following foods are rich in vitamins and minerals:

BREADS: Whole wheat, kamut, spelt, rye, corn, oat, or any combination are rich in complex carbohydrates, vitamin B complex, vitamin E, potassium, magnesium, chromium, manganese, molybdenum, selenium, zinc, fiber, and unsaturated fatty acids.

CEREALS: (Same as breads.) The best are whole rice, rye, wheat, oat, and corn grains.

DAIRY: Unprocessed cheeses, milk, yogurt, cottage cheese, eggnog, goat milk and cheese, kefir, and ice cream are rich in protein, fats, vitamin D (fortified), calcium, vitamin B_1, B_2, B_6, and B_{12}.

EGGS: The highest protein of any food. The yolk is extremely nutritious and contains lecithin, which keeps cholesterol moving through the bloodstream. Eggs include vitamin A, vitamin B_1, B_2, and B_{12}, biotin, choline, pantothenic acid, vitamin K, iron, manganese, sulfur, and zinc.

FATS: Unsaturated oils such as corn, peanut, safflower, sesame, canola, soybean, sunflower, wheat germ, margarine, and mayonnaise fit this category.

FRUITS: Fresh, canned, frozen, and dried. Most fruits are rich in complex carbohydrates, vitamin A, vitamin C, bioflavonoids, chromium, cobalt, iron, manganese, potassium, and fiber.

SEAFOOD: Fresh, canned, and frozen. Most seafoods are rich in unsaturated fatty acids and trace minerals. Tuna is exceptionally rich in minerals, amino acids, proteins, unsaturated fatty acids, vitamin A, vitamins B_1 and B_{12}, biotin, choline, folic acid, pantothenic acid, vitamin D, copper, sulfur, vanadium, and zinc.

POULTRY: Chicken, turkey, pheasant, and their organ meats. These birds are rich in protein, vitamin B_1, niacin, cobalt, and iron.

MEATS: Lean cuts, wild game, and their organ meats. These animals are rich in protein, vitamin A (liver), B-complex vitamins, vitamin E, cobalt, iron, molybdenum, potassium, sulfur, and zinc.

NUTS AND SEEDS: All kinds are rich in unsaturated fats, vitamins B_1 and B_2, inositol, copper, magnesium, manganese, potassium, zinc, and fiber.

VEGETABLES AND LEGUMES: Fresh and frozen. Vegetables should be steamed or sautéed lightly to preserve the nutrients. Drink the liquid in which your vegetables are boiled. A lot of nutrients are in that liquid. Rich in complex carbohydrates, vitamin A, PABA, folic acid, vitamin C, vitamin E, vitamin K, cobalt, copper, iron, magnesium, manganese, molybdenum, potassium, and fiber.

Now that you know more about foods and their nutrients, eat well, drink plenty of water, and take a multivitamin.

FIT FOR LIFE

Women today want faces and bodies that reflect their inner strengths, and the most important part of looking good is being healthy and fit. The way you feel will most assuredly reflect in the way you look. This I know for certain because I'm athletic. I can't remember a time when I wasn't leaping through the air in a *pas jeté*, running track, hiking, pumping iron, or teaching yoga, aerobics, or ballet.

Although exercise is individual, every person needs to find a type of routine that works for her. Be it three times weekly or more, exercise should be as much a part of your life as eating or sleeping. You can't imagine how good stretching, sweating, and working your muscles are for your state of mind and the maintenance of your body, not to mention your emotional stability and confidence.

I see girls and women walking into ballet class as if they were carrying the load of the world on their shoulders. And they probably are. After an hour-long class, not only do they look better physically, but their attitude is more positive and inviting.

Also, I have my own theory that a woman carries around a lot of excess water in her system that most definitely affects the way she feels and thinks. A woman actually has more fat cells than a man, and fat cells hold water. Once the water is expelled through perspiration, the woman is a different person. I see it all the time, especially with the women that I train. They walk in my door cranky and bitchy, and after an hour of working out on the StairMaster and with light weights, they're smiling. They like themselves again. Their self-respect takes a giant leap.

Looking good is a consequence of feeling good. Exercise will increase body awareness, correct bad posture, add energy to life, bestow a more youthful appearance, enhance sleep, boost the immune system, and help the remodeling of bones, thereby warding off osteoporosis. Because of exercise and good food, my waistline measures the same now as it did in high school. I am without a doubt in the best shape I've ever been, both physically and mentally. My diet is better, and my cholesterol and my body fat are lower. I like my maturity and the wisdom of my years, and I'm certainly more confident. I strongly urge you to try what has worked for me!

I work out every day, but most people don't have the time. So I suggest at least three times weekly, thirty minutes to an hour during each session for noticeable results. If you have a regular routine of Jazzercise, dancing, tennis, fast walking, running, swimming, stationary bicycling, or climbing the StairMaster . . . good for you! You're already ahead of the pack in the game of life.

STRETCHING

Stretching is a natural exercise that should be practiced regularly—a *must*. Stretching increases both your energy and endurance levels. Once the energy is flowing through your body, you can begin your workout. A few reasons for stretching are: to stimulate circulation; to rid your body of stiffness; to relieve aches and pains; to loosen up ligaments, muscles, and joints; to increase coordination and suppleness; and most important—to prevent injury.

When you stretch your muscles, you make them long and limber. Your body movements will become more catlike. The way you walk and handle yourself will be more elegant. You'll have more flexibility and feel more confident. So don't even think about working out without stretching first. Okay? *Muy, muy, importante*. The first thing I do when I wake up is to stretch out like a cat. It feels good. Watch how a cat stretches sometime, then imitate him—stretch and then get out of bed.

Before you begin your exercises, *prepare* for stretching—walk around your area. Never stretch cold. Hold each stretching position about thirty seconds before you move on to another one. After you complete your exercises, cool down by walking around. I lift my legs up one at a time for several minutes while walking. I'm sure I look like a prancing show horse, but it works for me.

Of all the various exercises I've done and still do, I believe ballet to be the very best for my particular body. Not only does it create beautiful legs, a tight derriere, a small waist, and an erect posture, but it bestows immeasurable grace. The music is classical, romantic, and soothing. Classes are focused and disciplined and the result following the effort is a heightened sense of well-being. You can always spot a ballerina. The femininity is undeniable.

My training schedule begins at my ballet barre. I do pliés (gradual bending of the knees with the body erect) in counts of four (four down and four up) for about ten minutes or until I break a sweat and feel sufficiently warmed up.

I start with a demi-plié (or half bending of the knees), before graduating into a grand plié which is a full bending. When I am traveling, I use a chair or windowsill to hold on to. This exercise renders the joints and muscles soft and pliable and the tendons flexible and elastic. It develops a sense of balance, and it maintains your body's correct posture, which is to say straight and proud.

At the barre, I always make sure that I hold my stomach in tightly, tuck in my buttocks, roll my shoulder in a circle—forward, up, and back—and hold my head up straight and tall. This allows a full inflation of my lungs, facilitates my concentration, and helps me focus on my exercise regimen.

Create the mood you want with music. Use whatever sound you need for motivation. I work out to current hits and my old faithfuls Tina Turner, Prince, Donna Summer, Sting, LL Cool J, or Deep Forest for isometrics, weights, and stomach crunches. For stretching and ballet I prefer Chopin's nocturnes or Erik Satie's *gymnopédies*. A good rule to always remember: concentrate, don't force moves and don't jerk. Everything nice and slow and smooth. Tummy in, butt tight, shoulders back, and head up. The best time to exercise is one hour before you eat or two hours after a full meal. You can't work out in a dizzy or weakened state, so don't skip meals. You defeat your purpose. If you feel lethargic, eat a piece of fruit an hour before exercising for sustained energy. Carrot juice is also very stimulating. It's best to wait thirty to forty-five minutes after a workout before you eat. Your body needs to come down from the exercise.

Break your body in slowly. Your warm-up is just to get the blood flowing, nothing else. It gives your muscles time to adjust to their new activity. Be careful not to overdo. Being excited and motivated is great, but forgetting to warm up and doing too much too soon will definitely cause injury—perhaps a torn muscle or ligament. Caution is the key. Be sensible with your body and heed the motto "Train, Don't Strain!" The first few times, expect sore muscles. That means they're waking and growing. Soreness is a good sign. Soaking in a hot Epsom salt bath helps soothe soreness.

BREATHING

Don't forget to breathe! Inhale when your body is under the least amount of pressure, exhale when you have resistance. When there is any strain, breathe out. Deep, regular breathing helps your blood get its maximum supply of oxygen. Your exercises will be easier and you will feel better as a result of more oxygen flow in the blood. Breathing right will also keep your mind focused on your goal. Be aware of your body posture. Incorrect posture could restrict your breathing.

SKIN

Vitamins A and E and zinc and betacarotene are great for the skin. They help rejuvenate the skin cells. Don't neglect any body part. The skin on your body is just as important as the skin of your face or hands. It should be given equal attention. Moisturize every inch of your beautiful self.

The most effective time to moisten your skin is after a hot bath or shower when your pores are open and ready to receive nourishment. Your cells need rejuvenation—out with the old, in with the new. For youthful, satin skin, keep a brush or abrasive sponge in your shower or bath to scrub off the old cells and make room for the new.

For many years, I have lubricated my entire body with either Nivea cream or coconut butter. I brush the dead cells off my skin in the shower and immediately smooth on Nivea while I'm wet.

When I travel, I buy an organic product of the country. In Hawaii, I use coconut oil; in Tahiti, I use their tropical combination. And if I happen to be in a country where I can find an aloe vera plant, I manage to cut it and squeeze the juice all over my body and face. It's the best!

When I lived at the beach, my girlfriend Kristina would come over for a ten-mile run to the pier and back. One morning, we decided to try a natural moisturizer. It was seven o'clock A.M., and we didn't think anyone would see us, so we plastered honey all over our faces. I suggested we wrap our thighs in cellophane to sweat more. We did. All the way to the pier there was not a soul in sight, but on the way back . . . guess who we ran into with honey dripping down our shirts and stuck in our hair and cellophane hanging around our knees? Bruce Willis, who was taking his morning run. Totally embarrassed, we ran the rest of the way home looking down, trying to hide.

I no longer live at the beach, but I believe a few minutes of sun now and again supplies the skin with the necessary vitamin D conversion. It also relaxes the nerves and soothes your mind while the sun's rays caress and penetrate your being. The sun's healing power for the soul is one of God's luxuries that doesn't cost a dime. But if you abuse the gift and bake yourself, you could end up like a portrait of Dorian Gray, which is to say, much older than your years. Again, moderation is key. A little color is nice and healthy, too much color is asking for trouble.

Sunblock goes wherever I go. I never walk out my door without using sunblock on my face, neck, and hands. Have you ever noticed that a woman's neck and hands age quicker than any other body part? That's unfortunate, since we use our hands for everything and our neck is always visible. The skin loses collagen and elastin, the chief constituents of connective tissue. Their depletion leaves the skin looking dried and shriveled. Unless you protect your hands by wearing rubber gloves when you clean and frequently use moisturizer all through the day, your hands will look well beyond their years. Many men have told me that they can tell a woman's age by the condition of her hands. So a word to the wise: keep your hands protected and nourished.

Well-manicured hands and feet are so appealing, especially for those men with foot and hand fetishes. Treat yourself to a manicure and pedicure from time to time. Or do it yourself on a weekly basis. If you don't know how, learn from a professional. Since skin grows over the nail bed daily, soak your cuticles in warm water until they're soft enough to push back. Then oil them. For a healthier maintenance, file them in a square shape. (A natural product for the growth of healthy hair, bones, and nails is Alta Sill-X Silica.)

Treatment for my face consists of boiling a pot of water, adding a tablespoon of Swiss Kriss, which is a herbal blend that draws out impurities, putting a towel over my head for a more concentrated effect, and steaming for a few minutes. I remove the towel and splash my face several times with cold water to revitalize and close the pores.

For a mask, I use either egg whites, milk of magnesia, or cooked oatmeal. All three tighten the skin and draw out the impurities. Then I wash off with cool water.

Soap never touches my face. Instead, I use Ponds cleansing cream, Abolene liquefying cleanser (which can also be used for sex), cocoa butter, Noxzema, or Neutrogena to remove makeup and cleanse my face. Then I take a warm cloth and wipe again. For a moisturizer I use either Kiehl's, Elizabeth Arden, Oil of Olay, or Derma Centre, depending on how I feel, and I am always willing to try something that might be better. I always cleanse my face and use a moisturizer before going to bed at night. It's a rewarding habit that reaps great rewards over time.

Tiny wrinkles are called laugh lines when you're young and crow's-feet when you're older. Why, why do the eyes wrinkle? Because the skin is so thin and oftentimes dry. Without moisturizer and sunblock, it resembles a fish's scale. It's important to invest in a good eye cream. I have tried many brands, but La Prairie produces the best results for me. I must warn you, it is expensive. Lamentably, I can only afford it a few times a year, so in place of my favorite cream, I puncture a hole in a vitamin E capsule and spread it around my eyes. It's most effective. And speaking of E, I also use vitamin E oil in a bottle, 10,000 IUs for my breasts and neck, with remarkable results. Emulsified Vitamin E will penetrate the skin most effectively.

HAIR

Your hair is usually the first thing people see. It should be nourished and cared for; and having healthy and fit hair need not be a chore. Beautiful hair flows, is vibrant, and dances in light and shadow. After all, it's your crowning glory. However, you must wash it regularly and use a good conditioner, or it will end up being your worst nightmare.

My girlfriend Debbie changes the color and style of her hair more than she changes clothes. When she greets me at the door, I'm always surprised. One day she's a blonde, another day she's a brunette, and today, she's a redhead.

Last week, she came over crying. The color of her hair had three different shades of blond and the cut was . . . well, I could have done better blindfolded. Her hairstylist was having a bad day and Debbie's hair was the result. When I saw her baked and fried hair, I had to bite my lip to keep from laughing. It was cartoonish. But after hearing of her misery, I was upset, too.

We discussed several solutions to her problem, one being, do it herself. What did she have to lose? She was well on her way to a crew cut. Her cut was choppy, the color was disgusting, and her hair was brittle and dry. We drove to the nearest pharmacy, purchased a rich auburn color by Clairol, and drove home to apply it. I cut off the dead ends, applied the color, a Kolestral conditioner by Wella, and voilà—a miracle. She looked beautiful.

Instead of spending your paycheck on your hair every month, if you're not quite satisfied, do it yourself from time to time. You'd be surprised how adept you can be.

I don't particularly like going to hair salons. In fact, I've probably been inside one four or five times my entire life. I don't fancy someone I don't know cutting and pulling on my hair. Once I had a devastating experience. My friends recommended that I visit a famous stylist. I made an appointment. He asked me what I wanted. I said, "Trim it a few inches, that's all." My hair was down to my waist, so a few inches was nothing. I closed my eyes while he trimmed. When I thought he was almost finished, I looked into the mirror, aghast. The hair to my waist was suddenly hair touching my shoulders. I stood up, speechless, instinctively reaching to the floor to clutch the last vestiges of my womanly mane. I learned a valuable lesson. Needless to say, that was the last time that I have ever let anyone touch my hair without first knowing them well and trusting them completely.

Luckily, I found a man named Jimie whom I now entrust with my crowning glory. Here are a few tips for the maintenance of yours: Lightly shampoo and condition your hair every day; if you have extremely dry hair, then every few days. But the most important thing is to keep your roots as clean as possible. The roots need to breathe and they cannot breathe if they are not clean.

While there are many high-quality "designer label" hair products for sale in salons and beauty supply stores, you can also get excellent results from products on your grocery store shelves that are far less expensive. While in the shower, I apply Wella Kolestral. It leaves my hair shiny, rich-looking, and extremely manageable. After rinsing the Kolestral, I use a dab of Pantene conditioner to prevent tangling. Oftentimes, I soak my hair with mayonnaise, wrap cellophane around my head, and ride the StairMaster for thirty minutes. Then I rinse and wash with shampoo. Mayonnaise, without a doubt, is the best conditioner for the money that you'll ever find.

If you have a problem with dandruff, there can be three causes: oily scalp, dry scalp, or nerves. If you have flaking, find out if your hair is oily or dry. Purchase a shampoo for your type of hair. Use a dandruff shampoo twice a week until your condition has improved. And for those of you who are starting to lose hair, you might try using the herb rosemary. It worked for my neighbor Susie, who was losing her hair rapidly. She took several leaves from a rosemary bush and boiled them in water. Every time she washed and rinsed her hair, she poured the brew over her roots. Months later, she had healthy hair. Remember—your beauty is uniquely yours—and needs to be appreciated and cultivated.

Using color can be tricky. Henna is a natural color and will not harm your hair, but you should never use it on bleached, white, or gray hair. It will turn orange or some ghastly color. If you have blond hair, use lemon juice for highlights. It turns blonder in the sun.

Remember, when choosing a style or color for your hair, stay true to who you are. Emphasize the positive you. A cut should emphasize the better qualities of your face. Don't start changing your hair, makeup, and wardrobe to please another person. You must please yourself before you will ever be able to please anyone else. Never copy what you see in a magazine on a model if you don't look exactly like that model, because you may end up looking ridiculous and ruin what good points you do have.

MAKEUP

Makeup looks better when it's sparingly applied to a clean face. The idea is to see your face when you are finished. I see young girls and women coming into ballet class during the first few weeks of the season with little or no makeup, and they are quite beautiful. Then . . . they spot a cute guy, someone they want to impress, and a transformation occurs . . . out comes the heavy eyeliner, heavy blush, a new hair arrangement, and bright red lipstick. The problem with mixing cosmetics and exercise or lovemaking is that lipstick, mascara, eyeliner, and base makeup can smear, smudge, and disappear—on your face, his collar, or someone's pillow. Your man may wonder if the girl he fell in love with the night before wasn't left on the floor or bed in the drippings of sweat. The point I'm making is that you can still be the irresistible girl who turned him on hours before by heeding a few simple tips for lovemaking.

Skin: Spot your base with a brush only where it is most needed. If you need to conceal blemishes, scars, or whatever, use a cover-up or concealer stick. (One with a yellow base is usually best.) Then use a loose, light dusting of translucent powder, especially on the chin.

Eyes: Avoid raccoon eyes by using waterproof or liquid liner, not pencil. Then brush on a smoky smudge of brown that runs through the creases.

Lashes: Enhance lashes by curling and using single false ones because if they fall off, he'll think they are yours. If you use mascara, do so sparingly.

Cheeks: Blush rosy circles on apples of cheeks, then powder again.

Lips: Trace lips, then fill in the center with berry pencil. Follow with lipstick or dab with gloss. Kiss and bite a tissue and lock on color with powder. When you're drinking wine, discreetly lick your tongue over the rim where you sip and your lipstick won't stain the glass.

Nails: Keep nails functional in length, clean, and polished pink. Red is to give ourselves a boost or for those wanton, passionate nights.

For parties: To fire up the night, add a bit of gold lipstick or gloss on center of lower lip. Use a lighter-than-foundation shade between crease from nose to mouth and frown lines. Play up eyes by using a gold shadow on outer corners. Put a bit of pearly highlighter on collarbone, on highest part of cheekbone, and under brow. A pale mauve powder can enhance your complexion as it evens out the skin tone.

One of the world's top makeup artists, Francesca Tolot, often works on Cindy Crawford, Demi Moore, Michelle Pfeiffer, Elle Macpherson, and many others. Francesca says, "Less is more." She doesn't create a made-up look, she follows a woman's natural features. One thing she always notices is that many women wear a base that ends under their chin, and it's usually the wrong color. It looks like a face that belongs to somebody else.

For lips, Francesca's trick is putting a little of the same base you use on your face in the middle of your lips. It makes them look fuller. For the face, she often mixes three different colors in order to get the right tone and achieve a three-dimensional look. Using just one color makes the face look flat.

Let me leave you with this thought: Makeup is a tool to enhance rather than hide. Your goal is to look pretty and natural rather than phony and made-up . . . except when you are role-playing with your man and you turn into a femme fatale. Or if being excessively made-up makes you feel good from time to time, go for it.

DRESS

Dress and style help determine how you will be perceived by the world and the man you want to win. Woman to woman, the future is about personal style; and a woman today is not shy about playing with styles in order to find her individual look. The look is more inviting because it is so diversified—individual, fun, and comfortable, from the androgynous to the ultrafeminine, sensual and romantic. It's be-true-to-yourself time! Your clothes should be a celebration of you. That's what style is all about.

The real woman dresses with inspiration and strength. She wears her clothes rather than having her clothes wear her. She appears free, together, and confident. She seeks the link between inner and outer expression.

Now let's discuss the basic difference between fashion and fads. A fad is a momentary look—a temporary style for amusement. If you're very young and a fad looks good on you, go for it. But most fads only look good on tall, thin girls.

I enjoy browsing the shops on Melrose Avenue and Hollywood Boulevard when I want to see the latest fads. Most of the people are amusing in their black leather outfits, chains, tattoos, bright-colored hair, and rings twisted in parts of their anatomy.

One day, I saw an attractive girl walking down the street with purple-and-green hair, a ring in her nose, black lipstick, black gloves with the fingers cut out, fishnet stockings with holes, and a skirt exposing a bit of cheek. I stood there aghast wondering, "Does she really think she's pretty?"

Fashion is simply a mode of dress that is currently prevailing in society. Keeping pace with fashion will make you look young and together. Being in style needn't be costly.

Accessorize! It only takes a few items every season to update and enhance your wardrobe. A new belt, a new pair of shoes, purse, scarf, earrings or necklace, or the current-style blouse and skirt. There is no greater advice anyone could ever give you than to keep it simple!

Don't wear anything that doesn't complement your body. If you have large thighs, you certainly don't want to wear a miniskirt. Miniskirts are for very slender and well-tanned legs—not varicose veins, sagging skin, and cellulite. When you do expose yourself, make sure it's the most appealing part of your anatomy. Don't enhance a large waist with a flashy belt or a large bosom with lots of ruffles. Large breasts require a more simple neckline. Ruffles are great on a smaller-breasted woman because they enhance her femininity. Selecting clothes and colors to emphasize your assets demonstrates that you are a clever and wise woman. If you don't know the most flattering line of clothes to buy and you don't know what colors are best for you, ask someone you admire to help you. It could be a man or woman who knows what looks best on you individually. Or if you've been complimented on certain clothes by several people, make a mental note and stick to the style that receives the most compliments.

And please don't make yourself over for a man. Similar to the concept of dressing for success: the idea of changing your look to suit a man's taste is yesterday's news, unless he knows more than you about style, fashion, and the cut of a suit. In a current survey, 60 percent of the women felt that by using the right clothing and makeup, any woman can be attractive to a man.

If your fella liked you in the first place, he liked you for you. To change yourself completely and present another woman to him is ludicrous. Your natural beauty is probably what attracted him to you. So again, accentuate the positive, play down the negative, and keep it simple.

In a memorable and beautiful scene from the film *Sayonara*, Red Buttons was yelling at and berating Miyoshi Umeki, the Japanese woman with whom he had fallen in love, because he discovered that she wanted to change the shape of her eyes to please him. She had made an appointment with a doctor who could cut the top eyelid in such a way as to enlarge the eyes, making them look more occidental. He told her that he loved her exactly the way she was and he loved the shape of her eyes. Miscommunication. The moral to the story is: if a man loves you, he loves *YOU*, not some alteration!

COMMUNICATION

A person who has really known the heights and depths of ardent lovemaking manages to communicate what he or she knows about it not only with every word that's spoken afterwards but with every intonation of the voice, every glance of the eye, every slightest movement of the arm or leg. The message cannot really be kept a secret.

—STENDHAL

"Please, Please, *please*, baby, *please*, do we have to talk about our relationship *again*?" is the familiar refrain of the typical man when you try getting him to sit down and communicate. Right? Instantly, the color of his face changes from a vibrant peach to a reticent white. He starts to sweat. His eyes exude that familiar, "How long is this gonna take?" He puts his hands in his lap, looks down at the floor, and waits . . . bracing himself for the worst.

What pain this so-called communication must be for that poor man. Did you notice that he manifested the same physical symptoms when you talked about commitment? These two claustrophobic C words, *commitment* and *communication*, make him feel put upon —as in loss of independence. A functional equivalent would be your right leg crunching his crotch.

A man listens differently from a woman. When you say, "We need to talk!" he's hearing, "Let's be honest with each other." He's upset; he feels his integrity is being questioned. How dare you question his intentions. Your confrontation of his feelings makes him feel betrayed. Even if you are right and he is double-timing you, he still feels stifled. He feels the ol' commitment thing recurring—claws going into his skin, anxiety level reaching claustrophobic proportions. His independence is being imposed upon . . . his power stripped.

A man is an adventurer: he likes to look out over the horizon and dream about what he can conquer; what he can do that's new; what he can tackle that he hasn't experienced before; how many points he can score on the journey. He strays from the present a lot.

There is a sense of adventure about his future and its possibilities that will never die; unless, of course, his spirit dies.

For you, talking is a release, an aphrodisiac. For him, it may be a drain, almost an insult. He thinks, "Now she's gonna drag me around by the neck for a while. I'm losing control of my life here!" And *control* is his middle name. It's the only ground where he truly feels comfortable.

When a man loses control, he loses his sense of maleness, which, in turn, makes him feel insecure. And insecurity can bring out his worst. He doesn't mean to be nasty, and he certainly doesn't want to hurt your feelings. It's just that he would rather be Comet Shoemaker-Levy 9 crashing into Jupiter than discussing subjects at hand. He generally thrives on short questions and short answers. He's a short fuse and you're a long fuse. That's all. Remember the cavemen, "Ugh, ugh, ugh!" Modern men are bottom-liners. Their mottoes: "Say what's on your mind in three words or less and move on."

Henry Ward Beecher was noted for saying, "The older I grow, the more I listen to people who don't talk too much." Most men don't object to giving the subject of "Relationship" a few minutes now and then. What they do mind is that those talks take too long and are not fun. Once aware, you can learn to be sensitive to that distinction.

When Napoléon Bonaparte was asked how he handled both the affairs of state and his personal life, he replied, "I compartmentalize. I open one drawer, fix the problem, shut it, and go on to another drawer and so forth. I focus only on what I am doing at that moment." And you, ladies, are asking your man to focus on a subject that's not within his manly agenda. He would much prefer fixing the engine of his car, adding another room onto the house, pitching balls in the backyard, or playing the stock market on his computer.

Most men deal with life in the above manner. They like to set specific goals and then accomplish them. They deal in numbers and wins. They feel a sense of pride when they finish a task or excel at a sport. So when you ask, "Can we talk?" it sounds vague to him. He can't see, touch, feel, or smell it. So he thinks, "What's the point?" and feels pinned down like a bug in a display case.

A woman's territory is uncharted land for a man. In the Brazilian Amazon Rain Forest, there is a section of land into which even the natives don't venture. They believe it holds forbidden mysteries. It's the same with men and the female language. They don't speak the tongue; therefore, they don't fancy dallying too long with it. Anything over five minutes and they get an itch. They feel themselves out of their habitat like a fish out of the water. The only reason—and I do mean *only* reason—a man will sit still for long periods while you have "the talk" is that he wants to please you, either for love, lust, money, or sex.

Only when passing through the initial stages of your acquaintance does a man actually enjoy and engage in lengthy discussions. He wants you to understand him and his needs. At this stage he tries to be a good friend, enabling him to learn if you can be a good friend in turn. It's the "getting to know all about you" stage. And because he knows little about you in the early part of your relationship, everything becomes an intriguing challenge—he's in competition for your attention. Therefore, communicating with you makes him feel good and it also justifies that level of your relationship.

Then, months later, you say, "Let's eat out tonight." He *thinks*, "Great! We'll go to Chuck's Steak House." You see, he already knows where he wants to eat and exactly what he wants to order. So you *think*, "I remember seeing a quaint little restaurant about five miles down the road near that English-looking cottage with the rose garden in front." You get in the car and he politely asks, "Honey, where would you like to eat?" You reply, "Oh, it doesn't matter. Wherever you like." You don't mean it, and he doesn't mean it, but you are both trying to be courteous to the other. Okay, you're driving for a few minutes and you say, "Why don't we go to that little restaurant we passed on the way home last Saturday night?" Now it starts. "What restaurant?" he asks good-humoredly. "Oh, you know, the one about five miles from here near that little cottage," you say. "No, I don't know!" Now he's getting famished. All he can think about is that steak. "Honey, can you give me a better idea, so we don't have to drive around all night?" he pleads. You retort, "Just drive. I'll know it when I see it."

What we have here is a failure to communicate— a chronic dilemma. Thus begins the communication breakdown. Both parties become frustrated with the other. On one hand, we have a man who knows exactly what he wants to eat and where. On the other hand, a woman who knows only the general vicinity of the restaurant she wants. This, ladies, is the communication breakdown. He's focused. She's not. Her spectrum is broad and filled with intriguing nuances. His is staccato, spasmodic. He's the bass—boom, boom, boom— who, what, where, when, why, and how. She's the melody—the flute drawing air from the heavens and flowing through the universe.

A classic example of our male-female directional differences is humorously depicted in the beginning of the film *The Bridges of Madison County* when Clint

Eastwood drives up to the house of Meryl Streep and asks for directions to a certain bridge. As Meryl explains, the quizzical look and smile that crosses his face is a picture worth a thousand words. She finally decides to hop into the truck and guide him there. Great, great moment!

A woman wants novelty, excitement, and romance in her life, smelling the lilies and breathing in the fresh air. A man focuses on one thing at a time, mapping out his course in space and logic. But remember, your melody not only has a beginning and an end; it also has a focus besides giving beauty to the rhythm of his bass. So tune your thoughts. When he asks you where you want to go—be ready and say, "A quaint little restaurant that serves great Italian food, but let me direct you there." Be affirmative. Unequivocally state where you want to go. And he will drive you there. Being clear will not diminish your mystery, but it will greatly reduce his frustration.

The bottom line is this: learn his likes and dislikes and try not to tax his tolerance level. Be honest. If you take him shopping, tell him that you want to spend some time at the store browsing. Then, if he agrees, he will go knowing what to expect. That's good!

Be straight and up-front with your man. Be kind. Be flexible. He's trying. Give him credit. Respect his preferences and needs—and he'll open up his heart to you in time. You're not going to change him, but you can encourage him to grow.

True love involves negotiation and compromise. Make a friend, learn how to be still, and properly listen to his needs with your kind heart and disclose yours. Give him time to absorb it all. He'll get there if you're patient and gently lead the way, instead of forcing him with manipulation to be something that he's not.

In compromising, you must understand his field of

concerns. We've discussed his hobbies. And, of course, a man's job will always be a top priority: it's his first wife. You must learn to be the mistress at first. His work is an extension of who and what he is. The success at his job may be one of the reasons he's got you—the woman of his dreams. His success and ability to provide might have been one of the key points on *your* list.

Another compromise is in appreciating his need for male bonding, which translates into his time spent with "the boys." Obviously you are also a very big part of his world, but he needs to fraternize with his buddies from time to time. You must be sensitive to his moods . . . and to his compartmentalized way of thinking and living. You need your space—give him his.

Every relationship has three different entities—your life, his life, and both of your lives together. One, you need to have your own interests aside from his. Two, he usually has his separate interests. Three, you both have common interests, and ideally your relationship flourishes when you mutually explore new and inventive avenues together.

Men get bored quickly, so you'll need to keep your connection to each other alive, active, and interesting. Remember that communication takes place through many different channels, and you need to optimize each channel because each also has its limitations.

In communicating with your man, remember that he always hears "your music" much more than "your words." So *how* you say things is just as important as what you say. For example, "*Larry*, we need to *talk*!" As you stress the word *talk*, your body language, the tone of your voice, and your inflection may indicate to Larry that you're upset, uptight, and about to dish out unpleasantries, in which case he recoils and prepares himself for the onslaught. Now, let's take the same sentence and make it more inviting. "Larry, could I have five minutes of your time? I really need your advice about the food we're serving Friday night." As you ask the question, your body language is free and open, the tone of your voice is calm and collected, and your inflection is confident. Therefore, Larry is all ears. He wants to be of assistance because you've come to him with respect—you've opened the door to true *love*.

Your body language should be in unison with the tone of your voice and your actions. They complete your female symphony. Words coupled with appropriate body language and inflection are very powerful indeed. Without the complete chorus, it's analogous to a doughnut without a hole or a Twinkie without the filling. How you make use of each setting will determine whether or not you flourish in your relationship, in your job, in your life. Be consistent and unwavering in your attempts at "loving communication."

Once you accomplish this, he'll look forward to these little talks just as enthusiastically as he listens to his male friends.

A man needs to know that he can trust you no matter what. And his trust is hard to earn. So once you have earned it, take care not to lose it. Keeping your word is the foundation of good communication.

Couples communicate in many different ways. Some share every fleeting thought. Others, like Glenda, thirty, and Joel, forty-one, have a strong relationship because they *don't* share too much. Glenda said, "I'm something of a risk taker and Joel is not. But the fact that we're so different makes our marriage a challenge. Because of our jobs, we spend a lot of time apart. We both enjoy brain sex, teasing, challenges on the phone, and when we do come together, sparks fly. He thinks I'm mysterious and I like that. Everybody should have secrets. It adds spice to life. I continue to be the seductive individual my Joel was attracted to. And he contin-

ues to be the inquisitive scientist that I fell in love with.
We don't feel the great necessity of long, drawn-out
conversations. However, when something is bothering
either of us, we come together and find a solution."

Whether you choose to share every thought or keep
a bit of mystery in your relationship is your call. Some
plants thrive in shady areas while others need direct
sun. Every couple must find what degree of shade (mystery) or sunlight (openness) is the best environment for
their relationship.

When out on a date with the hunk of your choice,
delicately try to uncover the important aspects of his
character. But do not, for your sake, launch an inqui-
sition:

"How are your parents? Do you keep in touch?"

"How did they treat you growing up?"

"Do you have brothers or sisters, and are you in
touch?"

"What kind of relationship did you have with your
family?"

"How did the other kids at school treat you?"

"Did you have fun in high school?"

"What are your memories of growing up?"

"Were you tall/short and how did it make you
feel?"

"When were you first attracted to girls?"

"Are you a late bloomer?"

Granted, these are good questions if you're sincere
and you've known him for a while. However, if they're
all on the first date, he may become suspicious that
you're working an angle. Yes, you absolutely want the
information. But it's much more effective if you make
an effort to be charming and show him that your interest in him is genuine and lasting. Ask your man a
few penetrating questions and he'll be flattered by
your interest. Conduct a third degree and he'll think

that you're nosy, insensitive, and rude. (And he'll be right.)

A common language on the subject of intimacy is still a mystery to both men and women. We approach it from all angles, but the feeling of warmth and caring that emanates is the same. So it's up to you to gain a better understanding of what your own intimate desires signify to you and what they mean to him. Then communicate what you want. Sometimes, a woman just needs a hug while she's cooking. Nothing more. Sometimes, a man thinks that a hug is a prelude to sex. If that's not the way you feel, tell him. He wants to please you. How will he know if you don't tell him? But don't just tell him. Explain why you are hurt—communicate. It's possible that he may be unaware as to how he disappointed you. Be patient in learning his ways while he's learning yours. And respect each other's differences—differences of gender, psyche, hormonal influence, and social background.

Males typically like to communicate about work, sports, craftlike hobbies, politics—physical or intellectual things. Women, on the other hand, gather their strength sharing intimate or emotional issues. So, ladies, initiate an open line of communication with your man by setting a few ground rules *in the beginning* of the relationship upon which you both agree. Set clear ground rules so he can please you better. Tell him what you want or don't want. Play by these rules and be happy. It takes two to tango, and sometimes one has to bend over backward to accommodate the other. Sometimes it's you, sometimes it's he who must master the art of bending.

If you begin by telling the truth about your feelings, it will lead to honest communication, thereby giving your man a better idea of who you really are. If he is craving Greek food, but you're dying to eat Thai, then suggest Thai. If he recommends a book for you to read, but you know in advance that you won't enjoy it, explain why. If he wants to see a certain movie, but you have either already seen it or you know for certain that it's not your type of film, say so. The point is stand up for yourself in a gentle, charming, and respectful way. Finally, it's good to know what you want, know when to ask for it, and also know when to give in to the moment at hand. Be open to give and take. This "dance of truth" will keep your relationship alive and real for as long as the two of you are willing to follow these steps.

COMMUNICATION TIPS

The Power of Words

A careless word may kindle strife;
A cruel word may wreck a life.
A bitter word may hate instill;
A brutal word may smite and kill.
A gracious word may smooth the way;
A joyous word may light the day.
A timely word may lessen stress;
A loving word may heal and bless.

—Unknown

Listening is the first rule in good conversation. You learn very little by talking, especially about the man you're with. You can learn only when you *listen*. If you're interested, you become interesting.

Try to empathize and relate. If you get a chance, watch Larry King and Oprah Winfrey. Pay close attention to these interview experts—how they listen to their guests. They hear every word that's spoken and they are keenly attentive to body language. They appear to really care and relate to what their guest is saying and feeling. All the good talk-show hosts listen more than they talk. They also ask poignant questions that help bring out the true personality of the guest.

Eye contact is your greatest ally in communication. It will tell your partner everything he needs to know. Talk with your eyes. It's sexy, mysterious, and pro-voc-a-tive. Some of the greatest female stars on the silver screen spoke volumes with their eyes alone: Greta Garbo, Marlene Dietrich, Lauren Bacall, Bette Davis, Barbara Stanwyck, and Merle Oberon to name a few. Rent some of their films and watch carefully how expressively they talked with their eyes. You'll learn a lot. When you're at a party, on a date, or dining with friends, always maintain good eye contact. But please don't stare. That's rude. It makes a person uncomfortable, unless your goal is playing a Bacall with Bogart. Otherwise, make eye contact frequently while out with your partner and don't look over his shoulder at all the handsome hunks that grace the place. That's insecure behavior. If you don't want to be with a particular man, don't be with him!

Always, always share your *sense of humor*. If you can make a man laugh, he will open up to you in ways you never dreamed. Men adore women who can make them laugh. With laughter, they can relax, be themselves, and forget about performance anxiety. Haven't you ever noticed that most of the truly great men in the world are not with the most beautiful women? They seem to gravitate toward attractive, smart women who have good energy and a terrific sense of humor. Langston Hughes said, "Humor is what you haven't got when you ought to have it." How true it is.

But having a sense of humor is not enough if the

other person doesn't get it. Your humor must be transmitted by making your partner aware of it, either by word or by gesture. Laughter will be your friend at any time, any place. And keeping a sense of humor will get you through the night. Laughter is an aphrodisiac. It removes all darkness and brings in the light.

Be aware that everyone has a different sense of humor. I often watch Mary Matalin on CNBC and Jane Wallace on FX. I love their wit. Mary's is a bit cynical and dry. Jane's is hearty and robust. These ladies never fail to make me laugh whether the subject is politics, human interest, or the weather. Because of their humor, I'm more interested in their subject. You can gather more admirers with honey and humor than vinegar and sarcasm.

At a party: what to talk about. Parties are difficult at best, especially cocktail parties. I hate small talk. Don't you? It's boring, but one must learn a few essential conversation starters or be left in a corner . . . alone. First, look around the room and assess the crowd. Awareness . . . remember? See if you can spot a small group of people who look inviting rather than clannish or snobby. If you see a friendly few (or one will do), walk up and listen for a few minutes. Maybe a person with manners will try to bring you into the conversation. Otherwise, pick a key moment when you feel secure and confident to join the subject at hand, either by adding something pertinent or asking an intelligent question.

For example, if the group is talking about the hottest new movie, you might add what you found interesting about a certain scene, or if you haven't seen it, ask the group what they found interesting about it and why they think you should see it. It could be a discussion about a popular book. If you have read it, tell your point of view, and if you haven't, ask others to describe theirs. The same applies to a variety of subjects such as politics, real-estate, the arts, the stock market, and even business.

One of the best ways to coax a person into further conversation is to be genuinely interested. Demonstrate your sincere interest by asking follow-up questions. Then contribute an observation that shows you have been affected by what has been said. For example, I hear daily that someone is moving out of Los Angeles, and I usually know the reason. But I'm still curious and pursue the line of inquiry in order to advance the conversation. Oftentimes, answers that are expected become more interesting by sheer elaboration, but also each person has a different point of view on any given subject that I find quite stimulating.

Most all human beings have something engaging to offer, if you just give them a chance. And people, in general, love to talk. So don't be afraid to get the ball rolling. When you graciously supply any person with the opportunity to express himself, you will be *remembered*.

Chapter 2

••

What Men Want . . . And Don't

Licence my roving hands, and let them go
Behind, before, above, between, below.
  —JOHN DONNE,
    "TO HIS MISTRESS GOING TO BED"

WHAT MEN WANT

But I, being poor, have only my dreams;
I have spread my dreams under your feet;
Tread softly because you tread on my dreams.
—W. B. YEATS,
"HE WISHES FOR THE CLOTHS OF HEAVEN"

Usually what you think men want is not what they really want. In fact, what *they* think they want is not what they really want either. In the musical film *My Fair Lady*, Rex Harrison as Professor Higgins wonders why women (specifically, Eliza) can't be more like men (more specifically, and ideally, him). Higgins can understand men and their actions and their thinking, but he is genuinely perplexed by Audrey Hepburn's Eliza Doolittle, the woman with whom he has unexpectedly fallen in love.

On a bet and with Henry Higgins's instruction, Eliza turns into a beautiful, desirable, and educated woman. Suddenly, Professor Higgins's world is topsy-turvy. But she, too, has fallen in love with him and she wants more . . . a commitment. The metamorphosis is devastating to him. He wants everything to return to what it was before—when *he* was in total control and secure. It can't. Eliza has developed into a woman with her own independent mind; and he, therefore, must accept the change and take responsibility for their relationship. It's a tall order, but in the end, he matures, professes his devotion, and all is happy.

A man wants you to love him for who he really is and not a fantasy of what you want him to be. He's not perfect. Face it. Nobody is, but he is the same person you fell in love with and he can get close to some of your wishes if you only give him a chance. Make that a few chances, because it takes time for him to interpret your agenda.

Dispense with thoughts of your fella being insensitive and unloving. That's not true. He is sensitive; he is loving. He just expresses love differently from you—so differently that you might not be aware when he is expressing love.

We identify and respond in different styles, different dialects. If you didn't speak French, wouldn't you be hard put to understand when a Frenchman was desperately asking you to open the car door, because you just slammed it on his finger? You could obviously see that something was amiss, but you might not be able to see his finger in the door for the first few seconds. My neighbor Keith did it to his dog. The poor dog was wailing in pain before Keith realized that the dog's tail was caught in the closed door. In turn, a man just wants you to take a few minutes and try to read the interpretations before reacting critically to anything he does. For this, you need to become "bilingual"—fluent in his style of communicating and your own. You see, we've had this habit of miscommunicating for centuries; and now, we are finally making a conscious effort to improve at one another's language. There's a lot of hope in this possibility. It does work. But only if both partners are willing to spend the rest of their lives in so doing.

A man does not wish to be categorized with other men. He wants to be an individual. He wants you to appreciate that he's not like the man next door. Or your favorite movie stars. He doesn't have the body of Arnold Schwarzenegger, the face of Mel Gibson, the charm of Kevin Costner, the ruggedness of Clint Eastwood, the sensuality of Antonio Banderas, the style of Denzel Washington, or the humor of Billy Crystal—he's simply himself and wants to be appreciated *for* himself, that's all.

Calling a man a sexist—*just because*—is wrong. Maybe he appears to be a sexist outwardly, but that does not necessarily mean he is one. Because of a man's conditioning, he has a different outlook on life, habits that constitute who he is and what he thinks. He probably learned this behavior from his father (if, in fact, he had one when he was growing up) or an uncle, grandfather, or other major male figure. He may not know any better. So don't accuse him of being a sexist until you investigate the situation thoroughly.

It's unrealistic for a woman to expect a man to react to love and sex in the same way she does. His senses of seeing, touching, smelling, tasting, and hearing do not respond the same way yours do. To begin with, he sees things differently from you. His mind is more compartmentalized and geared more toward the visual, the mechanical, and the nuts and bolts of a thing and orienting an object in space. The two of you can look at the same object, and I can almost guarantee you will see it differently. You are more likely to notice subtle variations of color and texture, while he will tend to see its shape and size. If you share your observations, you will be surprised at how different they can be. You might even wonder if you and he were looking at the same object. Try it sometime. It's fun. But more important, you'll gain more insight into his character. *Observe!*

Second, his sense of touch is a bit more aggressive than yours. Even though he's gentle and tender, he may often seem more overtly assertive. (Testosterone, you know—that driving force!) Just observe the way the male gender plays with an infant. Different! I've seen my friend Andy toss his kid in the air and I nearly had a heart attack before that baby was back in his arms. Whew! What I thought was a close call was just daily behavior. Not all men play with their children in this way, but many do.

Smell and taste fall into similar categories—he may find certain things ravishing, while you may think they're rancid. It's almost as if men have different olfactory systems and palates installed. I've watched my fella drink milk that was, let's just say, past the date on the carton. He didn't even notice that the milk was a bit sour. He drank it anyway.

Furthermore, a man tends to hear dialogue in sound bites—in "bottom line" terminology. If you're going on and on explaining how your can opener works, he's thinking, "What's the point? Get to the point already!" That's his reaction to lengthy conversations that travel in circles.

Men also tend to speak unvaryingly, unwaveringly, without taking many pauses; and oftentimes, they get loud when expressing themselves. Their oversell is usually due to the sheer excitement of wanting to impress you, and you guessed it . . . testosterone! An example: I have a friend named Don, whom I dearly adore and would do anything for, but Don goes on so. He could be talking to a ficus bush for the little I contribute to the conversation. His enthusiasm tends to run unbridled, and once he gets on a roll, look out! I feel like a cheerleader again, "Go, Don, go! Go for the touchdown!" Since I care about him, I've suggested that he relax and breathe when he talks. He's a wonderful person; it's just that his enthusiasm is a bit overwhelming. He has taken my suggestions, and his communicative skills have improved immensely.

If you have a similar problem, explain to your man that you would understand him better if he would take a few more pauses and lower his tone before continuing. And, in turn, you practice to be open and positive when listening to him and trying to get your point across. That's the key.

Women tend to speak in varying tones and take a lot of pauses, usually asking, "Don't you think?" (I do that one a lot!) "Isn't that right?" "You know what I'm saying?" or "Shouldn't we?" Men, on the other hand, use "umm" or "well" as a filler to formulate a thought. Neither sex has the market cornered on filler phrases. But men, categorically, may assume that you're either looking for an answer or some kind of approval, when actually you're just being nice by trying to involve them in conversation.

We're not really asking a question with our spicy phrases, do you think? We're speaking in female tongue, using both sides of our brain. It's how we relate. It works. Why not use the same technique for the opposite sex? Because it doesn't work, that's why. So, bottom line: Men want us to make a conscious effort to relate in their tongue when addressing them by speaking a little more solidly. You know, the way they do! Clarity of speech is a win for everyone.

These men obviously have a valid point: If you want to be heard, you need to speak the male tongue. It takes practice. When you wish to make a point, lower your pitch, raise your volume, and stick with the topic at hand. They'll love you for it; and, of course, they'll hear you every time. Another sound practice is to praise your man and give constructive advice on how to remedy a situation. Think before you speak. Don't criticize.

Jerry, thirty-two, a bank clerk in a Boise, Idaho, said, "I want a woman who can not only tell me what she doesn't like, but who can also offer some good suggestions as to fixing the problem. I'm not a mind reader. I can never come up with a solution that makes her happy. I don't like being told that something's not working. Just tell me how to fix it."

Another bit of sound information toward relating: it's really hard for a man to sit and listen for long periods of time, unless you're entertaining him in a way he enjoys. For example, when I give talks to a group of men, I carefully observe their body language and the expression in their eyes and on their face. No matter how interesting you think your subject is, they may not. Even when the subject is fascinating, most men have a difficult time sitting still for too long. They start to fidget; then slump in their chairs; then yawn; then look around; then look at their watches; and then . . . you've lost them! Before it gets to slumping-in-the-chair time, I try to do and say something exciting to once again capture their attention. It usually works, but it's challenging to continually shift when they shift. It takes a lot of energy.

Once you are more aware of male-female styles, you can amend your behavior patterns to fit his—a natural talk mate will appear, seemingly like magic. We all have a different point of view on any given subject. So we must try harder to understand the other's point of view. By watching his body language and listening with trained ears, we will be on the road to a better understanding of the masculine sex.

Now, there are those few who will think anything you say or do is interesting and exciting. They will hang on every word you utter, every motion you make, believing every nuance makes perfect sense. Conversing will be like slicing butter. But that's uncommon. And bless those chosen few!

The language difference between men and women extends to the expression of humor as well. Male humor is generally a tad brash compared to the more gentle female humor. They don't mean to be offensive; they simply perceive the world differently from you. Their style of humor often involves teasing you verbally, kidding with you like kids play in the backyard, jostling— a few pokes in the ribs, an inoffensive shove, an elbow wherever it reaches. It's a man's way of showing acceptance. He likes you! (You might think, "Please don't like me so much, I need that shoulder!") And when he clamps down on your knee in jest with iron fingers that cause paralyzing pain, he's only kidding.

In their small talk, men prefer talking about external things—sports, politics, current events, late-night talk shows, or their job. Women prefer to tell funny stories or reveal something personal—maybe even a secret. When a man makes a remark that he obviously thinks is funny and you find somewhat odd—pause— reevaluate. Rather than responding angrily, recognize it for what it was meant to be and accept it. Smile and go on. Don't sweat the small stuff when there are greater things awaiting your attention.

So much of understanding another person involves the simple consideration of his point of view and his circumstance—turmoil included. Ronnie, forty-eight, a playwright living in Hoboken, said, "I want a woman who values my work. As a writer I might go for months without making any money. I can manage if I budget properly. I don't need a woman to make snide remarks when I'm out of work, put down my manhood, and make light of my profession. I may seem selfish and egotistical, but I love my work, and the amount of income it generates at a given moment is not the only measure of its value. I want a little respect for the hard work I do and loneliness that I must endure in order to succeed." He's obviously come into contact with too many women who measure a man's worth by the money he brings home. A woman of quality would understand that talent, integrity, discipline, and hard work are attributes to cherish and praise, and will most likely lead to stability and comfort.

Kenneth, twenty-six, an oil rigger from Santa Fe, had this to say: "I don't want my wife to make me responsible for her happiness, nor do I want her to tell me how much she's sacrificed for me and the kids. If I hear the word *sacrifice* one more time, I think I'll stay in Saudi Arabia and never come home. I do plenty of sacrificing, too. She doesn't realize that I hate being away all the time. Living on planes is no picnic. She shouldn't make me feel guilty for what I can't do. I can only do so much. There's nothing wrong with a little encouragement once in a while. It sure would help." What a shame that Kenneth's wife was so involved in her own situation that she failed to see and appreciate what a heavy load her husband was carrying. She should have been his greatest cheerleader, not his most vitriolic critic.

Mike, thirty-one, an insurance salesman from Chicago, declared, "My wife is always complaining that I don't bring home enough money. I do the best I can. Some months are slow. I come home to a dirty house most of the time—dishes in the sink, clothes all over the place. She could pitch in, too. Even if she took a temp job, it would help. If you love the other person, you do your part—whatever it takes, right? I mean, if I was playin' baseball all day, sure she'd have a right to complain, but I'm busting my ass on the street trying to solicit customers. Most of the time my feet are killing me and I'm dog tired. And what do you think she's doing when I get home? Painting her toenails and watching soaps, that's what she's doing!" Mike is frustrated that his wife isn't holding up her end of their partnership. They're in a rowboat together and she's not pulling her oar. Neither one of them will get where they want to go if she continues to behave like a passenger.

When one partner crosses over the line of what's right and what's wrong, what's fair and what's not, then the other one will eventually balk. "I've had enough!" So either you do something about it or you get out. It's essential to know that a relationship is a lot of give-and-take, but mostly giving. It's never fifty-fifty. Sometimes it's sixty-forty. Sometimes it's eighty-twenty. There will be times when you give more, and he takes more.

I know guys who only give forty percent all the time, and they actually think they're giving sixty or more. One spouse will always do more than the other. But people shouldn't "keep score." Keeping score erases love. Giving should be a joy and receiving a pleasure.

The more I listen to men today, the more I realize how hard they try to understand us and give us what we want, in their own way. They often appear like Forrest Gump bumbling around in a dark closet and coming out with one shoe, but how are they expected to know anything on the female level if nobody taught them?

A man's behavior patterns and training have been passed down through centuries. The manner in which he acts and reacts is spontaneous to his training and behavior patterns. And retraining involves a lot of time and patience on everyone's part—yours and his. Luckily, the willing men are getting the message, but they need time to absorb, filter, and process. Their masculine map-reading minds are busily at work investigating the puzzle of our female needs. They definitely deserve an A for effort because there are too many men who never have tested and never will test the waters. Consider your man exceptional if he has the desire to please, to investigate, to try. Bless his heart, his body, and his goodness!!

MALE PSYCHE—HOW MEN THINK AND WHY

—chemical structure of testosterone

Ahhh . . . men!!! Why do you think men do what they do? What do you think makes a man behave in that foreign way that has eluded us for years? I've asked myself that question many times. After studying descriptions by psychiatrists, psychologists, physiologists, anthropologists, and social scientists who described the male psyche to the nth degree, I closed the books, sympathizing with Lord Byron when he complained, "I wish he would explain his explanation."

The information I found was so intricate and technical, I was more confused than ever. So I decided to write this chapter in fairly simple terms—partly because I was curious myself, and partly because I wanted you to understand your own man or the one you would like to have in your life.

Unraveling the male psyche and all the ingredients of his potent porridge—his fabric, texture, smell, smile, walk, talk, ups, downs, ins, and outs—will certainly add some titillating pleasure, but let's get real. The essential distinction between a man and a woman can—first, last, and always—be summed up in a single word: *testosterone*.

It's important to know that even among scientific experts much controversy exists about the specific behavioral effects of this hormone. No wonder we're confused! Classic theory relates aggression with excess testosterone. On the contrary, recent studies by endocrine scientists from U.C.L.A. suggest that male aggressiveness is actually related to a testosterone deficiency. I, along with many other experts, believe that it increases the sex drive and makes one physically stronger. But who knows what the truth really is?

Dr. Collins, a gynecologist in New York City, explains how this chemical influences and directs a man's behavior: "A man wants to deposit sperm wherever he can, to procreate the species. Now, I look at the body as being a survival machine for the genes' DNA. DNA's primary function is to duplicate itself, and over the billions of years that life has been on earth, the tissue around the genes are just machines which enable these genes to multiply and divide. As far as males are concerned, they seem to have one basic function and that is to deposit sperm. The main function of the female is to receive the sperm. To reproduce. Anything else is our conditioning, our culture. Even marriage is a blending into society. Polygamy or monogamy—there is nothing right or wrong about it. It depends on how you were brought up, where, and your attitude. Men, basically, when depositing sperm, don't care who they deposit it with!"

Now that we've identified man's primary hormonal driving force, let's look a little further into the composition of his personal symphony. Other than his mighty testosterone, he's tuned to an amalgam of the society in which he lives, his environment, his culture, male peer pressure, parental expectations, formative nurturing, subjective goals, and, of course, let's not forget, his genes.

This concoction is directed by guideposts he uses throughout his maturing stages. Early in life he develops heroes, living or dead, that provide guidance for his growth. As he matures, the intensity of his aspirations does not change. It merely orients itself to more worldly events. Deep inside, he imagines his role in gallant, chivalrous ways. He lifts his goddess onto a marble pedestal and adores her. He sees her as perfect, wants her to be perfect, and places her image on the hood of his car, boat, plane, or spacecraft. He writes, sculpts, makes music, poetry, or just dances, or makes plain loud noises, with her as his inspiration. He carries her image in his wallet, his mind, and heart, and he tries to imagine how life would be in her company.

So he strives throughout his adolescence and manhood to grow, to learn, to be successful, to conquer it all, and then put it at the feet of this strange creature he loves—his ideal woman. But it's a struggle. He knows he has to mature and succeed first. All through that process of growing and striving for success, his relationships with women are very rocky, filled with ups and downs, with momentary successes and fleeting failures. If he does something right and succeeds, he wants to be close to her. If he has setbacks or failures, he pulls away in despair and solitude. Women should recognize these deep, inner aspirations instead of regarding them as unstable thought patterns. In so doing, she can provide the steady companionship that will foster his hopes and nurture them into a mature reality within a solid relationship.

Setting aside some of his deeper fantasies, you can begin to understand a man by discerning his distinctly male attitude toward life. There are several fundamental aspects to consider, but the most salient needs of a man are *RECOGNITION* and *ACCEPTANCE*. All the rest will fit into these two main categories.

A man must have recognition to feel that he's part of society. When he gains recognition, he needs to know that his family will affirm his credibility. These days, it's much more difficult than it was years ago. Then, the road to recognition was easier. It was more prevalent for both father and mother, working as a unit, to guide their son into a useful profession. Role models began at home in that less fragmented era.

Today, parents still influence their children, but innumerable divorces have loosened the foundation of family structure. Suffice it to say, there are an increasing number of obstacles involved in the happy integration of males into society. But given certain inherent aptitudes, a man can gear himself toward success at something—with one of his main motivators being the acquisition of recognition—even if that means role-playing.

If his true vocation coincides with the role, then he is whole and happy. But if he has geared himself toward a profession that is not attuned to his true self, he gains success and recognition, but then realizes sometime later in life that there is another self inside crying out for fulfillment. It's safe to assume that most men, in one way or another, are playing a role. They display two characters: one on the inside and one on the outside. The real person underneath will always be there, but he plays a role when confronting society. This may explain the seeming anomaly of the proverbial physicist who plays the violin, the architect who wields chessmen, and the statesman who strokes his paintbrush at the easel. They all have artistic impulses and inclinations which they've had to suppress in order to become successful professionals driven by a need for recognition.

So today's male plays a successful, professional role on the outside and for each friend, and for himself; thus becoming the complex triad of characters as explained before—the one he shows others, the one he thinks he is, and the one he really is.

Okay, ladies, here's where you come in. When a woman falls in love with her man and gives him acceptance, she gets under his skin. He feels and appreciates that she cares. Now you can see why the marrying woman doesn't have to be a sex bomb. She only needs to know how to please her man. She laughs at his jokes, even if she's heard them a hundred times; she *sometimes* fakes orgasms (as long as she has the real ones often enough), she coos on the phone when he calls, and sings his praises, saying, "Oh, how great, how intelligent." He feels accepted and loved. He needs it. Every man needs that acceptance. Every present he brings her she praises. If he brings one rose, she puts it in a vase, shows it off, smells it. She makes a big deal of his small gift and then the next time, he brings a bouquet of them. He feels accepted. He feels that he's done something right, so he makes progressively greater gestures. He does what he can to feel accepted.

And so, we see the same pattern within his social role. He studies whatever is required to be somebody —anything to be recognized. Then, after the recognition he needs acceptance. The potential trap is the acquisition of one without the other. There are many famous and well-to-do people, instantly recognizable, but totally miserable because they don't feel genuinely accepted.

What comes of this recognition and acceptance? It gives a man his *self-esteem*. There exists a harmonious integration of all three of these states that blossoms fully in the well-adjusted man. If you as a woman can understand that a man needs to feel good within himself, you will foster his self-esteem. This is the glue that helps bind your marriage. A woman of encouragement might say, "Look, it's going to be fine. You're striving.

I love you. We'll work it out." If she makes him feel good about himself, he should succeed.

However, even if a woman loves a man, but constantly nags at him ("Oh, you're wrong. Look at the neighbors. They're doing better than we are. Why can't we have a swimming pool?"), she chips away at his self-esteem. And that can trigger highly destructive behavior.

So if you're clever and caring and can bolster the self-esteem in your man by telling him "You're my hero," "I love you just the way you are," "Look how nicely you're dressed," "I like the way you smell" (or whatever else you find desirable and attractive about him), you make him feel good about himself and help raise his level of self-esteem.

A man needs to know that his heroine is standing in the wings watching him—doting on him when he comes offstage. She needs to praise him, to encourage positively: "You were great!" And when she's routinely not there, he eventually will find acceptance elsewhere. Please understand that helping your mate is in no way demeaning. His potency—physical, mental, and material—is directly related to yours. Your rewards are as great as his. And what wouldn't you do for your best friend in life?

Having examined healthy aspects of the male psyche—the need for recognition, approval, and self-esteem—let's explore some of the less savory aspects in order to recognize telltale signs, so that positive and timely action may be taken to ward off unwanted consequences.

The need to be right, even when wrong (très important): Consider the usual sequence of events at an automobile accident. Usually, regardless of fault, each party will accuse the other. Two people will get out of their cars and start yelling about the other's fault—not recognizing their own. "Look what you made me do! Your fidgeting distracted me and now I've hit a telephone pole!" The perpetrator knows he's wrong, but will still fight to accuse the other person. This behavior finds its way into contemporary battles when a lawyer offers the best defense in the form of offense, regardless of justice. This type of mentality is ancient—seeing the speck in his brother's eye when a plank is lodged in his own. So, girls, keep your eyes open! He'll be certain to appreciate the one woman in the world with eyesight good enough to see that he's right when everybody else thinks he's wrong.

The propensity to make false claims and/or coopt others' work (importare): In his continuing quest for acceptance and recognition, a man can brag undeservedly about accomplishments that are not his own. "Fish stories" are legendary. He falsely expands the day's catch from a few bluegills to a bag full of prize-winning trout. He can turn personal losses at a Las Vegas outing into an armful of blue chips. My girlfriend's husband boasted that he had shot an eight-point buck while hunting in Montana, but we discovered that he didn't even see one! Do you think my girlfriend let her husband know that she knew? Not a chance.

If a man buys something in the market, brings it home, doctors it up, and exclaims, "Look what I cooked!" he only wants to be your "hot fudge sundae" with a little admiration and acceptance sprinkled on top. Granted, many men who invent a life full of half-truths are bad eggs, but there are quite a few lovable ones who just don't know any better. My uncle, for example, was a portrait painter and jazz musician who never left Mississippi, but he told great stories of adventures that took him around the globe, and those stories gave joy to my aunt and the rest of us. Who cares that they weren't strictly (or even approximately) true?

A terrific example of coopting another man's heroics that you can visually enjoy is in the film *True Lies*. It was beautifully enacted by the actor Bill Paxton, who was trying to win the affections of Jamie Lee Curtis. He drove a red Corvette, imitating the real heroics of her husband Arnold Schwarzenegger, but his clever antics were humorously uncovered.

The distorted need for power (muy importante): Society is replete with examples of excess and abuse of power. Too many men are obsessed with a pathological need to control and/or "win." Remember the film *Dangerous Liaisons*, when John Malkovich dueled with Keanu Reeves over a mindless matter? This winning obsession was certainly not worth a life. But with the flick of a blade . . . finito.

Even when the results aren't fatal, these abuses can ruin reputations and careers as the stakes rise. In certain criminal circles . . . *whack*, your man may lose his "humdinger," or his life! Extreme examples, I agree, yet they can and do happen. So be sure to keep a close eye on your man and his manhood. Even when it's not in danger, it's worth watching.

The lack of humor, aka the inability to take a joke: A relationship with a man who lacks a sense of humor takes an extraordinary amount of hard work. Take some time to evaluate whether he's worth all that trouble before you take him on. A man who lacks humor may be unsure of himself or even clinically paranoid. If the paranoia is deep-seated, it may be unalterable. However, most men are less damaged and you can gently lead them to the lighter side of life by your own example. Inspire your man by taking your motto from Rabelais: "For all your ills I give you laughter," or simply, "If your man needs a smile, give him one of yours." Smiles can be as contagious as yawns, so share them.

Having reviewed some of the negatives of the male

psyche, it's important to realize that each of these defects manifests a need—a need to believe he's made the right decisions and taken the right actions in life; a need to be congratulated for his accomplishments (small ones as well as big); and a need to know you are aware of and even honor his male potency. I don't think that's asking too much as a price for lasting relationships, do you?

After all, don't they do as much for us? They'll even go so far as to pretend to not only admire but also follow our own eating fads. A while ago on a late night talk show, I once heard Alec Baldwin, the incredibly handsome, funny, and bright actor, admit that he sometimes "fakes about food" for his gorgeous wife. She's a vegetarian; so is he (except that once in a while, he gobbles down a few McDonald's hamburgers). Richard Gere, another terrific-looking and sexy actor, says that he has often played a similar gallant role with women: "If *she wanted* me to be a vegetarian, I *was* vegetarian. If she wanted me to eat meat, I ate meat. I would do anything to woo her. Then I would hide in my room and smoke cigars and go out with the boys for beer and steak." You see, we all extend ourselves to please one another, if we feel the prize is worth it.

Be careful here that you don't let your desire to please lead you to disguise, distort, or mutilate your own character and personality. In the long run, if you do not display your true colors, you run the risk of his falling in love with your disguise and not you.

For your part, study your man! Find out all you can about his good and bad traits. Look at them realistically and decide if you can live with his psychological makeup exactly as it is. Don't count on his changing. People never really change, they only alter a few habits—sometimes for the better, sometimes not. When you fall in love with a man, make certain you can accept his faults as much as you do his accomplishments. Because you will be living with both of them.

Once you've decided that you *can* live with his faults, don't emasculate him at home or anywhere else. Every time something goes wrong in the house—such as the plumbing, electricity, or construction—and he tries to fix it, let him! Keep your sense of humor, smile, and say to yourself, "I never did mind about the little things."

Remember that your fella wants to be your hero. So don't be too quick to call in the professionals. It's embarrassing for him and it's his house, too! Never sacrifice his ego for your desire to have things "perfect." For some reason, we tolerate atrocities from perfect strangers, pay more than eighty dollars an hour for aggravating incompetence, but refuse to endure inabilities in the man we love. Sound familiar?

If you love your man, back him up at all times. Protect him, praise him, and give him the respect he deserves. Respect his individuality, his privacy, his silence, his small victories, his mind, and traces of his soul that he leaves in all the "little things." Remember that he is emotionally fragile and he thinks of you as stronger even in your weakest moments. If you withdraw your support, he may, in his despair, begin to seek help elsewhere. And you know exactly what I mean!

LAST THOUGHTS

The evolution of a true romance is like an adventure. At the beginning there is almost a dreamlike state. The middle of an adventure is challenge and discovery. And at the end of this journey . . . elevated happiness. For a man, romance is the spirit of adventure. On the Barbara Walters show even the great John Wayne admitted to being a romantic. Men just need a little encouragement in this area.

Your man wants to be your Don Juan. It's a role where he is allowed to become more dramatic, more wondrous, more heroic, more chivalrous. It's also the most divine intersection where a man and a woman may find true union; where they may vibrate to the promise of the extraordinary. But unfortunately, a woman believes him the least in this dance of romance. Half the time, she thinks he's faking to get her into bed. Not true! That's just who he is. He's being romantic in the only way he knows how. Stay tuned in to him because he's anxiously waiting for the words: "Go slay a few dragons for me, baby!"

CLASSIC TURNOFFS

If you think you're outclassed, you are; you've got to think high to rise. You've just got to be sure of yourself—before you can win the prize.

—UNKNOWN

There are many women who are wealthy in assets and poor in love. Their days and nights are rife with disappointments—married men, men who disappear, men who are stalled in their careers or stalling in their commitments, men who tell tales and weave webs of deceit.

Why do you think these women live in misery and sabotage their own happiness for the wrong man? Either they don't like themselves and project an unattainable ideal onto the wrong man; or in their enthusiasm to turn him on, they inevitably turn him off. Wanting to please a man you like is natural, but turning every encounter into an event is a bit unnatural and a desperate approach.

Pause . . . take a deep breath—question your old approach—and be willing to change your old way of thinking. It may be time to take stock of your approach, attitudes, and behavior. See if any of the comments below sound familiar.

Never do the following to catch a man:

1. correct his grammar
2. do drugs with him
3. get breast implants
4. follow him
5. be too available
6. call him at all hours and hang up
7. criticize him
8. lie about how many men want you
9. change your appearance
10. try to appear smart while making him feel stupid
11. after a few dates, tell him you've stopped seeing others
12. sleep with him on the first date
13. starve yourself
14. spend all your money refurbishing your wardrobe
15. give yes and no answers to his questions
16. lose your identity
17. pretend to be something you're not

Simple don'ts:

1. Don't be like Glenn Close in *Fatal Attraction*. Michael Douglas was in serious lust until he realized she was nuts about him.
2. Don't be like Bonnie Bedelia in *Judicial Consent*. When she became suspicious of her husband, she fell into the arms of Billy Wirth, the first young, attractive man who chased her.

TYPES OF WOMEN MEN HATE
Winnie the Whiner
Motto: "I don't eat anything—I don't know why I'm so fat. My nose is too large, my hair is thin, I burned the dinner, and I have PMS!"

* is extremely insecure
* nothing is ever right
* complains for the sake of complaining
* finds fault with everything
* wants attention all the time
* is always depressed
* can't find a good man
* sends her dinner back, often
* always puts down other people
* thinks the world owes her a living
* can't make a decision
* blames everybody for her misfortunes
* puts herself down all the time
* looks for the easy way out
* doesn't want to work
* can't keep a job

Jane the Jealous
Motto: "She's a star because she's had plastic surgery done to every part of her body and she's married to the producer!"

* thinks she deserves the best without working for it
* is usually conceited
* whatever you've got, she wants
* can't stand to hear good news about another
* must be the center of attention
* is seriously insecure
* doesn't really like anybody, not even herself

- always compares herself to others and invariably wants what they have
- puts down anybody who is successful at anything
- is a real downer most of the time
- never trusts anyone, especially her man
- is suspicious of every woman and every man
- imagines the worst
- is overly possessive
- is usually phobic

Polly the Pleaser
Motto: "I know it's 3 A.M. and all the stores are closed, but I'll find you a chocolate bar somewhere if I have to drive to the next county!"

- is the first to volunteer
- is wishy-washy
- thinks she's boring
- allows her man to walk all over her
- is generous to a fault
- makes excuses for everything
- usually pays the check
- gives until it hurts without asking for anything
- lets the spotlight shine on everyone but herself
- is obsessed with doing good
- can't make a decision
- doesn't know where she stands on political issues or even if she liked a movie
- finds only men who take
- fools herself
- is a do-gooder
- is passive
- never argues or expresses her point of view
- doesn't know her point of view

Betty the Bitch

Motto: "Just watch me. I'll take her husband away from her without even trying!"

- is selfish
- is sarcastic
- puts everybody and everything down
- has an overblown sense of entitlement
- is always frustrated
- believes everyone should think like her
- can often be downright nasty
- takes over every conversation
- has a snide remark for every occasion
- thinks she's better than anyone
- is very angry
- will do anything to succeed—anything
- tries to change everyone
- fights, complains, blames
- is destructive
- is abrasive
- usually has no dignity or pride
- will do anything to look good
- demands a lot, usually does little in return

Cybil the Cynic

Motto: "Oh, yeah, right, he's really gonna go to the moon!"

- finds the worst in every situation
- thinks the world and all the people in it are doomed
- is pessimistic
- is sarcastic
- is always afraid
- has a sour outlook on life

- makes negative remarks
- is usually a hypochondriac
- is a frightened little girl inside
- invents reasons why she's rejected
- gives up too easily

May the Manipulator

Motto: "Look how I sacrificed for you and never asked for anything in return!" (just your life . . .)

- uses charm to manipulate
- cons everyone into doing what she wants
- inventories everyone's emotional buttons for later use
- pretends good deeds are for you, but it's always for her
- is a control freak
- needs to know everyone's business
- gives presents for entrapment
- does everything with a string attached
- tries to run everyone's life
- suffocates loved ones under the guise of love
- has fits of hysteria
- has no sense of humor
- is extremely jealous
- always does her good deeds for a price
- gossips big-time
- makes loved ones feel guilty if they don't do what she wants
- marries a man she can boss
- tries to run her children's lives

If you recognize yourself in any of the above when faced with a difficult situation, overcome the frustration, anger, or rage with constructive resolutions: recall the goals that you originally set for yourself. Think hard about what you really want. Close your eyes and picture yourself a winner—say, "I can," "I will . . ." And maintain your sense of pride by quickly doing something positive—take a walk and fill your lungs with fresh air; call a trusted friend; take five or ten minutes to reel off a few affirmations to yourself; read a pleasant passage, note card, or line of poetry that brings you harmony; play music that makes you smile; sing a song; exercise; speak lovingly to yourself: "I am a good person," "I will attract good, loving, and caring people," "I respect myself because I have accomplished a lot with hard work," "I deserve good things—a good man, a good job, a good life," "I will achieve my goals because I am focused and disciplined."

Women who are needy, anxious, and desperate to find Mr. Right are usually hearing their biological clocks running overtime; or they're lonely; or they want financial support. They're existing in an unlived life with an unrealized self-image. They need to apply emotional cosmetics by discovering values that have meaning for them, interests that involve activity, and enthusiasm for things outside their own egos. They need to find things to do by themselves and for themselves. That very neediness or anxiety or desperation to find a man communicates itself to a man as fear does to a dog. Just as a dog who senses your fear will be inclined to attack, a man who senses your anxiety and neediness will likely be turned off and run. And you will be brushing off the dust from his quick exit.

ROMANCE

A true love never tires or wanes but is with us always, like our blood, like our breath. I shall never weary of that brow nor those grey, wistful eyes.

—ABELARD TO HÉLOÏSE

More and more, men and women are returning to romance. Technological advancement, deterioration of the environment, deadly communicable disease, and ignorance of reality have catapulted us into a lonely, confused, valueless, and alienated state. We don't communicate enough on a human level anymore, so we turn to fantasy, romance, and surrealism as a substitute.

Look around. We are immersing ourselves in mechanistic fantasies and communication systems which distance us from reality. We're inundated with PCs, CDs, VCRs, TVs, CD-ROMs, cyberspace, cyber sex, virtual reality. Wow! Listen to those words! And now we've got interactive TV—talking to your television. How stimulating! Just turn on your tube for thirty minutes and channel-surf. You'll see that we have so numbed ourselves, nothing less than a stun gun to our heads will make us feel.

Today, we live out our relationships on talk shows and soaps. Beepers and car phones have taken the place of face-to-face relationships. There's rarely peace of mind. Someone is always beeping us on our cellular car phone or digital pager. We read less, we ponder less, and we interact with others less. We're surrounded and absorbed by the mechanical rather than the natural. We are slowly bankrupting our spirits as we rush to meet the future, expanding goals of technological "progress."

It's sad, but even our ability to distinguish right from wrong is eroding. In a *Los Angeles Times* interview, filmmaker-actor Robert Redford lamented: "There used to be a thing called ethics. And there was a thing called shame. It doesn't exist anymore, because corruption has become a way of life."

Of course, our modern tragedy is that we're losing our true purpose in life: living and loving, being honest and kind to each other, and tending the better angels of our nature. As we lose the awareness and practice of relating to one another, we turn to the illusory aspects of heroes and heroines, gods and goddesses—the fantastic, the mythic, and the beautiful. Lacking the human touch, we live vicariously through the symbols of media imagery, always longing and searching for the beauty of sweet romance—that realm of magic that transports us into the spiritual world where goodness, love, and hope reign supreme, forever bathed in human affection.

But what are we really searching for? Is it infatuation, romantic love, real love . . . or ourselves? That is the question. I thoroughly believe the answer lies in the happy combination of *all* these aspects of love. The attainment of true love in its highest form involves a natural progression which begins with infatuation, travels through a star-crossed romance, and culminates in real love. And along the way, we just may be fortunate enough to find the true essence of ourselves.

And yet, the road begins simply . . . with infatuation. Infatuation in itself is a trifling state. In fact, *infatuation* is defined as "a state of foolishness." But there's much more involved; it includes not only illusion and fantasy, but hope and a promise for the future.

A man gives you a glance. Hmmm . . . you've intrigued him. You're titillated, too! It progresses into good positive communication, and then . . . he asks you for a date. Yes! Finally! The moment arrives—he prepares himself nicely—he brings you a considerate little gift. He surprises you with a well-thought-out evening.

If the date goes well, he invites you on another one, or you invite him to a picnic or the theater. You soon discover that you are compatible—and sparks begin to fly!

The courtship commences with true and positive feelings, with no ulterior motives. You're just getting to know each other, finding out your likes and dislikes, your dos and don'ts. You give each other music, books, flowers, food, notes, candy, cards, tickets to special events—tokens of your affection as your relationship grows.

It leads to real commitment. As long as both of you grow in the same direction, it will develop into true love. Be sure to tell your man in a subtle and charming way what your feelings are. He can't possibly know if you don't tell him. Most men are not visionaries. So when your man brings you something thoughtful, express your appreciation, even if it's not exactly your cup of tea. It's important to encourage the romance in him. You need to show him that what he does is pleasing to you. That way you'll command the attention of *all* parts of him!

Now let's look at what we all love about love . . . romance. Romance is as old as time itself and is a form of behavior that can be traced from biblical times up to the present. The medieval era was especially noted for the celebration of "courtly love"—a chivalrous form of devotion that had its basis in the spiritual rather than the physical. Knights wooed their ladies by fulfilling service, worship, obedience, and idealization, but always from afar—always full of proper intention. They were never to suggest anything intimate or sexual; they could feel passion, but never consummate it. In this realm of the presumed ideal, love was never ordinary —always ethereal, self-effacing, calling for discipline, courage, and generosity. The fuel of the imagination was thus fed, giving rise to tales of legend, adventure, and chivalry. To this day we anoint our icons with the

Arthurian mantle. The Kennedy White House, steeped in elegance, culture, and grace, came to be known as "Camelot." Noble love has been the inspiration of literature for centuries, as evidenced by the following romantic verses:

Abelard to Héloïse: "Would that I love my God as I do you!"

Tristan to Iseult: "We shall go together to a fortunate land from which none return. There rises a castle of white marble; at each of its thousand windows burns a lighted candle; at each, a minstrel plays and sings a melody without end . . . what does death matter? You call me, you want me, I come!"

Romeo to Juliet: "Ah dear Juliet, why art thou yet so fair? Shall I believe that unsubstantial Death is amorous, and that the lean abhorred monster keeps thee here in dark to be his paramour? For fear of that, I still will stay with thee, and never from this palace of dim night depart again."

The power of the pen has amazing capacity. It can induce laughter or tears, praise or consolation. It is one of the richest allies of communication, just as beautiful Héloïse described to her lover: "What cannot letters inspire? They have souls; they can speak; they have in them all that force which expresses the transport of the heart; they have all the fire of our passions!"

It is fortunate for us that despite their innate delicacy, letters have endured. How many of us can be transported instantly to another time through a letter? Long after a conversation has dimmed, we can recapture the full blush of feelings by rereading our letters . . . or those of our predecessors. Family chests are full of such treasures. My own chest is filled with love letters from my mentor, the late sage and writer Henry Miller.

As an avid letter writer myself, I urge you to pick up your pen and communicate with your loved one or sit down at your computer and send him an E-mail. If you prefer, confide your thoughts to your own diary. You will be able to communicate feeling and thoughts that you could not or would not do on the phone or in person. Not only can you enlighten, persuade, console, compliment, fantasize, and love, but you can also turn an average affair into one of passion and romance.

With all its heroism and inspiration, the "fairy-tale" romance, steeped in fantasy, is destined to fail. Overwhelming lust and haunting passion remain unreal unless two lovers can accept one another as individuals and want what is best for the other without selfishly clinging. And what is best oftentimes means parting. Unfortunately, our attachments often latch on so tightly that they suck the living breath from both parties as they run wild and unbridled, straight into disaster. The intensity of their passion is enough to make them believe in a life of eternal ecstasy with no peace, no sleep, no food, and no thoughts that aren't of one another. These lovers would rather die than be apart for one moment. This is selfish love. When separated, they have no patience to wait. In true love, people can be separated by war, disease, or death, and wait years and years or a lifetime for each other.

Yes, it is wonderful to journey into "fantasy love," as long as you know that romantic novels, romantic stories, and romantic movies are a beautiful escape— not a reality. Most mythical lovers were "in love with love," not necessarily with each other. I've certainly been "in love with love" before I was actually in love with the man himself—flaws, foibles, and all. Haven't you? It's great for the very young, but it goes nowhere.

It can't; it's not real love. Only real love can last for an eternity—imaginary love is simply an idealistic projection.

When you're in fantasy and you think you're in reality, you're actually in confusion. A wise woman knows the difference and uses fantasy to color her world, not to confuse it. Your key is knowing the difference.

A strong caveat: *Beware the romantic user!* The romantic user will provide you with plenty of fantasy, but he will use your romantic sensibilities for his own needs. He will always be attracted by the thing he doesn't have, the place he hasn't been, the girl he hasn't met. Once he wins you over, he becomes bored, and off he goes to the next conquest. Sound familiar? He's a parasitic evil knight looking for a new paramour; and the wide-eyed innocent, longing for love and romance, is the one he will mark for his prey.

The "too good to be true" romantic man will take you to parts of your brain you have never visited and make you feel as though you were having a religious experience—a divine ecstasy that excites your molecules and titillates your rosebud. When this same "too good to be true" romantic man sweeps you into his arms and carries you up the steps of his marble castle, with melodious music filling the air and white candles lighting the way, he is spinning his magic spell by intoxicating your every sense. You are temporarily invited into a dream where he reigns supreme. He will put you on a pedestal and worship you as his queen—until you wake from your dreamlike trance and seek a commitment. Then he'll be hitting the high road to China.

Only the most hardened woman would fail to succumb to such pure magic. The way he describes a restaurant, a day, the weather, a particular event is colored with spectacular flair. He beguiles you. You wait, breath bated, until the moment he will occupy the same space with you. He learned the art of romance from every woman he encountered because he pays attention; that's his job. He captivates the emptiness of your soul with his mysterious images, his attentive charm, his colorful conversation, his transformation of the ordinary into the extraordinary. His "magic wand" perfumes the air with drama (and enlivens the bedroom with irresistible alchemy!).

He *is* your knight in shining armor, if only temporarily. He fills your vacuum with vision, but he usually lacks soul and substance to back it up. He's simply a figment of your imagination—a projection.

And because it's a selfish love, it can only destroy. So a comedy of errors ensues: a lack of commitment, empty promises, canceled dates. You know the rest.

He takes his leave of you, tramples on your love, and flits to another ingenue who yearns to lose herself in his elusive advances. He's a one-man show; a pro at dealing fantasy and illusion. And by living in fantasy alone, he's unable to graduate to a level of maturity. His relationships remain mysterious and childlike, which is fun for a while, but they cannot last. Inevitably he leaves you with a broken heart and plenty of self-doubt.

So if you happen to fall "in love with love," and with a man who takes you on a magic carpet ride of unrealistic visual beauty . . . don't stop to think, *run*! This man is unable to reveal his true self, because the "self" is missing. The actor in him is a superlative and opulent delight, but the man is an emotional retard.

No one can maintain insatiable passion, devout charm, and intense adoration for too long. Intense emotions at a fever pitch are unnatural. But they can lead to love if you guide them properly. If a man is true, his romantic endeavors will be directed toward commitment and a lasting relationship. All of his actions will make good sense. He will have forgiveness, understanding, care, concern, and compassion. He will look beyond the externals and see only the beauty and goodness in you—for he is your "knight in shining armor."

To avoid getting caught in an illusory web woven by an "evil knight," you must respect yourself, even if that means redefining your values and changing your old patterns. *Don't deceive yourself!* Infatuation without an afterlife is a lonely life.

Ask yourself the big question: "Is he gonna be there when the going gets tough?" Hard times are getting harder. You must stay away from that endless journey toward the perfect man, the perfect relationship, the perfect marriage, the perfect friendship, the perfect job, the perfect diet, the perfect table setting, and the perfect penis. Because perfect means entirely without fault—flawless. I certainly don't know anyone without a defect. Do you? In fact, defects can actually be charming. Think of Clark Gable's large ears. It added to his strength of character and made him appear more manly. Sly Stallone's lazy bottom lip does not prevent him from being a great kisser, as Sharon Stone will attest.

The point I'm making is don't be blinded by outward beauty and brawn. Look to a good man who is worthy of your devotion. Search for someone who's at home—his door open, his smile inviting, and his fireplace crackling with the fresh smell of real wood to warm your hands and ease your heart.

Yes, life should include passion, a positive attitude, and a vivid and active imagination. And I will strongly encourage hopes and dreams and fantasies. We desperately need them. But it is unhealthy to live only in your imagination. You need to experience the beauty of life with a complete person who can give love as well as receive.

There are men who instinctively know the art of true and meaningful romance, but they are uncommon. If you find one, nurture the relationship. Never lose your own sense of giving, caring, and romance—moonlight, candlelight, champagne, roses, little thoughtful gifts, poetry, music, lovely scents, sensual foods, eroticism, a walk on the beach holding hands, sitting on a mountain watching the sunset, sharing an ice-cream cone, or appreciating nature together. You can keep real love alive long after the initial infatuation and heated passions fade.

Here are some off-the-cuff romantic notions:

- writing love letters and love notes
- kissing the nape of the neck and shoulders
- getting caught in a snowstorm
- a late supper of cheese and champagne
- leaving love and sex notes in a trail to the bed
- sharing hors d'oeuvres and desserts
- sleeping nude
- erotic lingerie
- a feel under the table at a divine restaurant
- outdoor comfortable sex
- a garden café
- a bunch of handpicked wildflowers
- falling asleep spoon fashion
- surprise gifts (a book, CD, music box)
- flirtatious looks across a crowded room
- slow dancing
- walking in the rain
- waiting a long time for sex
- wearing a part of his clothing
- a marriage proposal

- long, lingering, seductive kisses—anywhere, everywhere
- a warm hug
- touching your face tenderly
- phone calls just because
- thoughtful gestures
- inventiveness—ingenuity to make something unexpected out of nothing.

Remember: age has no bearing on romance—on the enjoyment of things shared. These experiences should be nourished and cultivated. Romance is a simple way of celebrating the beautification of the senses—seeing, touching, smelling, tasting, and hearing.

True love: What does "true love" mean to you? Saint Paul, who is not generally thought of as a romantic figure, had a real handle on the subject. We learn from him that love is unconditional; patient and kind; never jealous; never boastful or conceited; never selfish or rude; never offensive or resentful; ready to excuse, to trust, to hope, to support, to endure whatever, and will last forever.

Eighteen centuries later, Elizabeth Barrett Browning gave us a feminine perspective:

How do I love thee? Let me count the ways.
I love thee to the depth and breadth and height
My soul can reach, when feeling out of sight
For the ends of Being and ideal Grace.
I love thee to the level of everyday's
Most quiet need, by sun and candle-light.
I love thee freely, as men strive for Right;
I love thee purely, as they turn from Praise.
I love thee with the passion put to use
In my old griefs, and with my childhood's faith.

I love thee with a love I seemed to lose
With my lost saints.—I love thee with the breath,
Smiles, tears, of all my life!—and, if God choose,
I shall but love thee better after death.

Love is the sunshine of the soul. Without giving love or being loved, we grow old and bitter. Love colors the world in vibrant hues and gives us a reason to be happy. It sweetens distasteful experiences and softens jealousy and selfishness that is also intrinsic in human nature.

When true love guides your actions, the ego is not important; the well-being and protection of the other person is. We value and honor their worth as a human being, are considerate of them, care for them, and support them for who and what they are.

Love inspires loyalty. Henry Miller, writer and sage, used to say: "Love is complete and utter surrender. That's a big word, *surrender*. It doesn't mean letting people walk all over you, take advantage of you. It's when we surrender control, let go of our egos, that all the love in the world is there waiting for us. Love is not a game, it's a state of being."

In conclusion here is one of the most profound and beautiful expressions that any man could ever give to a woman. I cherish this letter from Henry and share it with you in the hope that you will understand what it meant and still means to me.

May 29, 1980

And now, . . . madly in love with a young woman who writes me the most extraordinary letters, who loves me to death, who keeps me alive and in love (a perfect love for the first time), who writes me such profound and touching thoughts that I am joyous and confused as only a teenager could be. But more than that—grateful, thankful, lucky. Do I really deserve all the beautiful praises you heap on me? You cause me to wonder exactly who I am, do I really know who and what I am? You leave me swimming in mystery. For that I love you all the more. I get down on my knees, I pray for you, I bless you with what little sainthood is in me. May you fare well, dearest Brenda, and never regret this romance in the midst of your young life. We have been both blessed. We are not of this world. We are of the stars and the universe beyond.

Long live Brenda Venus!

God give her joy and fulfillment and love eternal!

Henry

Chapter 3

How to Get Started

SETTING THE STAGE FOR SEX

She walks in beauty, like the night
Of cloudless climes and starry skies;
And all that's best of dark and bright
Meet in her aspect and her eyes.
　　　　　　　　　　—LORD BYRON

Napoléon Bonaparte is the greatest conqueror of all time, but do you know who conquered him long before Waterloo? The exotic Josephine. Do you know how? By using the art of seduction, flair, panache, intelligence, and an eye attentive to detail, Josephine beguiled Napoléon's senses. No other woman had captured both his heart and male member quite so passionately—and for that, he crowned her empress.

One thing we can say about Josephine . . . she was *prepared*! Preparation for their lovemaking was a lavish production. She made it her business to find out all of Napoléon's likes and dislikes. Her choices were his choices. She planned the romantic interlude using all of *his* favorite objects, which appealed to *his* senses. Doing it for herself would have defeated her purpose.

When Napoléon arrived for an evening, she would have his favorite incense smoldering through the air, perfume generously sprayed onto chaise longues, candles burning in chandeliers and throughout the house. Rivers of flowers strewn from the front door, up the staircase, into her bedroom, and finally covering the bed where they lay. His favorite champagne iced in solid silver served in fine crystal glasses. The powerful aphrodisiac of music could be heard from a concealed room where several musicians played the music of his choice during the entire rendezvous. Erotic books were cleverly placed within view. Of course, food for his palate was on display everywhere his fingers could reach. Napoléon was famous for soaking in a tepid tub for hours, and Josephine would always have one ready—just the right temperature—filled with exotic oils and bubbles.

The final touch was Josephine, herself. While Napoléon soaked, Josephine would dance. Wearing only Napoléon's gifts . . . rare jewels, silks, and satins, she displayed her naked body for his pleasure. She screened her velvet skin with transparent, diaphanous fabrics while she seduced. Her breath, sweet like the nectar of succulent fruit, laced their conversation with compliments, witty remarks, news of the day, courtly humorous gossip, and always comments on his winning strategy in battle. She praised his efforts, she lifted his worn spirits, she bathed him, massaged his aching body with soothing oils, and loved his manhood on her sensual satin sheets. She treated him like an emperor long before he took the throne. That's how Josephine got Napoléon!

Cleopatra, queen of the Nile, was a little more risqué. For her true love Mark Antony, she contrived new ways to win his favors. Always swathed in the finest fabrics, finest fragrance, finest jewels, Cleopatra tantalized his imagination and his senses not only with her own divine beauty but also with a bevy of the most beautiful girls.

While lounging in her famous Titian pose, she would summon the pageantry to begin with a clap of her hands. And what followed was bloodred wine from her queendom to intoxicate Mark Antony's mind; plus a variety of exquisite-tasting foods from various countries, carried to the dining hall by muscular servants scantily clad in mere leather straps. Mixed in with these delicacies were other feminine lovelies, wearing only strawberries on their nipples and grapes on their fur. While dining, Cleopatra used her wit and cleverness to affect Mark Antony's ego. During the feast, a flood of highly sexual and erotic dances were performed with ecstatic energy. The exhibition began subtly, and built to a haunting frenzy. With plenty of spirits for his head, food for his stomach, eroticism for his eyes, and music for his ears, Mark Antony's senses had fallen madly in love with the ethereal lady.

My point in telling these tales is that one of the ways to a man's soul is through his senses—all of them: sight, smell, taste, touch, and hearing. Research his favorite tastes. Microscopically study his likes and dislikes. Maybe what you like doesn't appeal to his senses. The key is to make him feel comfortable and at home. Without prying, ask subtle questions about these particulars and pay close attention to what he doesn't say. The most important point: set the scene for *him*, not yourself.

The *right mood* can make an evening. The wrong mood can end in disaster. Color and lighting should be your first concern. Inquire about his favorite colors. If he finds certain colors offensive, don't wear them. A good rule to remember is that men tend to like whatever reminds them of nature. Colors like red, orange, and yellow remind a man of fire. The "language of love" is embroidered with the theme of fire—hot, passionate, smoldering, sizzling, burning. Fire is alive, dangerous, mysterious—the burning of embers . . . dazzling—forever changing a lover's mood. One of the most erotic nights of my life was in front of a blazing hearth. Bodies and faces look more attractive in the glow of firelight, candlelight . . . moonlight.

Creating a mood does not cost money. You need imagination and a few trade secrets: candles, music, exotic oils, delicacies for the palate, champagne or wine, and your sexy self. With little effort, parasols, rattan screens, sheer curtains, artistic pictures, and plants can also create a dramatic effect.

Even though many men often say their favorite color is blue, blue lighting is not flattering when setting a romantic mood. For romance, your skin should look like a *Playboy* photo. The photographers at *Playboy* make the girls look gorgeous by using orange filters over their cameras. You can manipulate the same effect for your skin by buying orange filters and putting them over your lamps. You'll be amazed how the flaws disappear. Or if you prefer candlelight, put all shapes of candles in your living space. (Don't depend on a single candle to light your face.)

Soft lighting, in general, is flattering to the face; red lighting casts a sexy, decadent effect; floor lighting sets a theatrical mood; and dim lighting behind a palm tree is seductive. If you're making love under a full moon in a secluded garden or your own backyard, nothing else is needed. The moon creates its own mystique.

After appropriate lighting, you need appropriate sound. What about his sense of hearing? Does he enjoy silence or music? Although music is a powerful tool for seduction, use your intuition to gauge his momentary needs. Maybe he has a clambering headache from the noise at work and all he wants to hear is silence and the music of your voice.

Music, on the other hand, has the potency of a mind-altering drug for many people. The Institute for Advanced Study of Human Sexuality in San Francisco, California, rated music the highest of aphrodisiacs. Romantic music is certainly individual. That's why you need to know his taste. To your ears Edith Piaf's "La Vie en Rose" may be the sexiest ever, but to his ears it may sound like fingernails raking across a blackboard.

Without knowing his personal likes and dislikes in music, you can only go so far. However, I'll give you a starting place to look for the music that will excite him. If you know his approximate age, try out the romantic songs that were popular when he was in his high school and college years. More often than not, he'll find them very evocative. Also, music from his cultural and social background is a good bet. Test it sometime.

Watch your favorite romantic movie and observe. Maybe it's *An Affair to Remember* with Cary Grant and Deborah Kerr, *Gone with the Wind* with Clark Gable and Vivien Leigh, *Romeo and Juliet* with the young Leonard Whiting and Olivia Hussey, or *The Age of Innocence* with Daniel Day-Lewis and Michelle Pfeiffer. Turn the sound off and watch without the grandiose themes. Pretty bland, huh?

Think of creating a movie scene to please your lover. What he hears in the background while making love to you can either enrich his senses or distract them; and you don't want any distractions while trying to win his affections. So research the kind of music and the artists he listens to, especially his more sensual favorites. During lovemaking you want seductive and sultry sounds, not heavy metal, rock and roll, or rap.

Eliminate other background noises—telephones ringing, message machines clicking on and off, and a television blaring—while you're trying to win his heart.

The sense of smell is an erotic channel. Fragrant aromas can work romantic wonders on the olfactory receptors. I've noticed that more men comment on a woman's perfume nonverbally. When a lovely-looking, great-smelling lady passes by, a man's head automatically turns in her direction—following her with his eyes long after she's gone, while the scent of her perfume permeates his mind. Try putting a few drops of your perfume or favorite oil on a lit lamp bulb. The heat will disperse its fragrance over the entire room, right into his memory. I spray my perfume over my sheets hours before my man arrives, because men hate anything laden with heavy perfume and scents.

You must be very careful not to overdo. That can be distracting, too. I know the sweetest woman, named Addie, who believes that she once lived in the eighteenth century. Her house is filled with incense, scented oils, scented soaps, scented candles, and her scented self to the point where it is nauseating. She's thirty-eight and wants to marry, but unfortunately can't seem to find a man willing to tolerate the abundance of fragrance. Maybe she'll get lucky and find a man with an obstructed nasal airway. Don't overwhelm your fella with too much of a good thing.

Most men tend to like the smell of the outdoors. Fresh-cut flowers, plants, clean hair, and a freshly scrubbed body will turn him on (a dab of your favorite perfume on you and parts of your clothes). But whatever your choice, keep it moderate. When I was preparing a romantic packet for lovers for QVC, I included massage oils and lotions, soaps, incense, candles, robes, music, my S.O.S. book, and other items. Since it was a universal package, I tested hundreds of men's olfactory senses. Almost all of them preferred the less fragrant scents, the more natural-smelling ones. The richer smells seemed to make them grimace. But that doesn't apply to all men. So I suggest that you visit a bath-and-body shop with your fella and select scents that you both enjoy.

Your man's sense of taste should not be overlooked. Eating together is one of the greatest pleasures in life. It can be both sensual and seductive, depending on what you serve. First, find out what foods he likes and what foods he cannot digest. Some men have serious problems with indigestion. Take that into consideration when you display your delicious delicacies on a silver or glass tray. I don't know a man alive who doesn't enjoy a good home-cooked meal.

I spent several months in Iran once and came to understand the words of the medieval Persian poet Omar Khayyám, who gave us his romantic guide. "Here with a loaf of bread beneath the bough, a flask of wine, a book of verse, and thou beside me singing in the wilderness." Ask your man if he likes champagne and what his favorite vintages might be. Inquire about his taste in red and white wines, beer, brandy, and liquor. Some men only like dry martinis, others find the taste of fine champagne intoxicating, while some don't drink at all. In that case, you need to be inventive and serve him chilled and interesting mineral waters, sodas, or unusual fruit juices. Whatever you serve him, make sure it's what he likes.

The sense of touch can stimulate the release of endorphins—chemicals that change your moods. If he's as tense and nervous from a draining day at work as you are, mutually exchanged massages to the temples, neck, and shoulders will do wonders for you both! Use your fingers to relax his body and his mind. Try doing it rhythmically. The right rhythm can be hypnotic.

A complete body massage is heavenly. It's also a prelude to lovemaking and I will share techniques popular with seductresses and love goddesses in the next chapter.

The sense of sight is arguably the most significant erotic channel. Gazing into each other's eyes is so sensual. To appeal to his tender sight, you need visual stimuli in your home and on your body. For example: the book *Erotic Spirituality: The Vision of Konarak* is a healthy start. Each page is a wonder of sexual appetites and it's acceptable decor for your coffee table. Anyone who appreciates great art and hasn't previously viewed its pages is in for a treat.

Other sensual books by certain well-known photographers can also be a contribution to your scene-setting mood. Erotic statuettes strewn throughout your home stir attention. Mirrors in carefully chosen places are highly sexual. Subtle but provocative art hanging on your walls, fresh-cut flowers or roses in a vase, lit candles, a warm bubble bath, a large bed with lots of pillows and turned-down soft sheets are spicy for a night to remember. Be aware that there are a few extremely shy men out there. Insofar as possible, display your fine arts with his tastes in mind. You don't want to shock, you want to *please*.

Now for your person. You know he likes to look at you because you like to look at him. So give the hungry warrior something to look at. Dress with clothes that you feel comfortable wearing, but also keep in mind that they should feel sensual to his touch and be pleasing to his erotic eye. Whatever your assets, let them peek out but not fall out. Falling will come later.

Most men love stockings and garter belts, lace bras, tight or flowing dresses, clean shiny hair and body, well-kept fingernails and toenails (some men like red, some don't), a sweet mouth with no chewing gum or smoke in it (you can do that when you're alone)—in general, healthy-looking women who radiate happiness, and confidence.

If your man doesn't feel freer, more relaxed, rejuvenated, and turned on after all your consideration and fanfare, then he must be an alien!

WHERE TO FIND MEN

I do want to get rich but I never want to do what there is to do to get rich!

—GERTRUDE STEIN

Soul mate searching? He's out there. You may not even realize it, but he may be working with you side by side, or in the car next to you at a stoplight, or in a record store, or walking down the street headed in your direction. Don't be surprised. It happens! I was in Albuquerque, New Mexico, walking up a steep hill with my girlfriend Loretta, looking for some obscure restaurant that served good food. As Loretta spotted the restaurant, the most beautiful pair of sky blue eyes that I had ever seen walked out the door straight in our direction. I couldn't breathe or move. He stared at me, I stared at him, and we both felt like a bolt of lightning had suddenly hit us. Call it fate, destiny, karma, kismet, or whatever you believe. It does happen. Not very often, granted, but then it wouldn't be dynamic if it happened every day. Would it?

Your soul mate may even be the man next door whom you tease unmercifully, but because he falls short of your fantasy, you never open your heart to him. Take another look around you. By putting your mind back into your body, observing and paying attention to the little things, whoever and wherever *he* is, you'll soon see him. Maybe he's the guy who looks a little nerdy and wears glasses. Well, remember Superman? He acted a little nerdy and wore glasses. Look what happened when he took off his street clothes. *Mamma mia!*

My thirty-two-year-old friend Jamie, a cinematic art director, told me recently that she had fallen madly in love with a writer-director she worked with intermittently for four years. She said, "I never took him seriously, until we were working closely on the same film. Every morning we would find ourselves sipping coffee and laughing uproariously. He was so funny, my days passed in humor. We quickly discovered that we had a lot in common—the same sense of humor, artistic interests, music appreciation, and sensibilities. Coffee led to lunch, lunch led to dinner, dinner led to bed!"

Now they are blissfully intertwined. He asked her to marry him.

The bottom line is keep an open mind, be spontaneous, and maintain your positive attitude. When you need a pair of pliers urgently, rush off to the hardware store. You never know where he's lurking. Most fellas need hardware items. And so do you! Browse around auto supply stores and learn about your own car (how to change the oil, fix a flat tire, or enhance your car's physical appearance). Just ask some available hunk.

I met my man in an art gallery. We both appreciate art, so we had a lot to talk about. There are several art openings throughout the year usually listed in the local paper. Just put yourself together and go. You will always find someone interested in discussing art. It might be *him*.

Bookstores are definitely in fashion, even if you're not a great reader. There is always a good book you can find that will pique your interest. The library is an intriguing place for those of you who like to investigate. There is something very erotic about meeting a man in a library among all that time-honored knowledge.

I was primarily raised in the "rag" business and have watched people's behavior patterns while they shopped. For those of you who love to dress, you could easily meet the man who shares your fashion sense in a men's clothing store.

There are some women who love sports. Innumerable men hang out around athletic stores or places where baseball memorabilia is sold. Hobby and specialty stores in general cater to a variety of interests. You will find not only browsers, but hard-core collectors. And if you are interested, there is no better way to start a conversation than to ask a question. I happen to love old movies. A movie memorabilia store is a fun place to meet men interested in that subject. Men who are true collectors tend to be obsessed about their hobby. I have found that they are enthusiastic about discussing any aspect of their specific interest.

A while ago I enrolled in a computer class where I met several highly intelligent men. If you are computer oriented, then join a class. Computers are changing more rapidly than I can type. By the time you learn or buy the latest, you discover that an even more efficient system is on the market. Computers and software are endless, and you will find endless personalities from all walks of life who deal with these machines. Almost every person today either knows a bit about them or is an expert on the subject. Ask questions and learn from the lucky male.

Are you interested in gourmet food? It's amazing how many men are good cooks, many of whom enroll in cooking classes (probably looking for women friends!). I'm usually an average cook, except when I'm in love, and then I am exceptional. How about you? Doesn't love bring out the creative juices in all of us? As you know, food can be erotic and sensual. And obviously we need to eat, so why not make your gourmet delight for him?

Men involved with the preparation of fine foods are usually very sensual men. I've known a lot of professional men who are great cooks, but I've also known a lot of nonprofessional men who are superb cooks. The choice is yours. Walk through kitchen supply stores to buy your utensils. There is nothing more appealing and important than a variety of good, sharp knives in the kitchen. A kitchen without good knives is a kitchen without a good cook. Men who cook seem to be extraordinarily knowledgeable on the subject of knives. So when you see that "certain man" wandering around in the supply store, what better line of communication than to ask his advice on the best peeling knife? We all need one.

In health food stores, you will usually find healthy men. If you happen to meet a friendly face in the produce section, then make an inspiring comment about nutrition or ask a question concerning natural foods, juices, et cetera. Get the ball rolling down the aisles. Also, the same information applies at the larger supermarkets. Whether you're standing in line at the checkout stand or strolling your basket through the aisles, if you spot someone who captures your fancy, think fast. Say something innocent but clever.

Looking for a pet lover? We know women love pets, but so do most men. Men tend to love their dogs, especially the larger breeds. It's more fun for a man to roughhouse with a dog half his size than a toy-sized terrier. They can both playfully unload their aggressions. If you own a pet, you will obviously need supplies from time to time, right? Plan on spending more time than necessary at the pet store some day.

What about the Laundromat? I can't tell you how many young actors and actresses, secretaries and businessmen, musicians and music lovers, doctors, lawyers, and Indian chiefs meet at the Laundromat. You can tell a lot about a guy when you watch how he does laundry. How he folds or throws his clothes in the basket. The type of clothes he wears. Yes, indeed, you can tell a lot about a person at the Laundromat, if you're so inclined.

When I eat out alone I often take a seat at the

counter. If you are not in a hurry, eating counters are intimate and fun because there are usually other interesting people dining at the same counter. The same applies to sushi bars. I have noticed that men in general prefer eating at the counter than sitting at a table, especially during breakfast or lunch. So if you want to meet a beauty, don't stick a book in your face while you're nibbling. How is he gonna see your beautiful face when it's buried in a book?

Nowadays there are more men jogging on tracks and at parks, especially on the weekends or early mornings. I've jogged most of my life and can attest that a track surface is easier on your joints than the pavement. If you're a jogger, I don't need to tell you anything you don't already know. If you're not, and you want to meet a fellow that's fit, then put on your shorts and sneakers and start running toward that piece of passion that you can't resist. A word to the wise: don't wear jewelry and a lot of makeup. That turns the athletic type off.

I taught aerobics classes a few years ago, and I usually had more men than women in my classes. But if you don't find what you're looking for there, wander through the gym into the weight room where all the Herculean types congregate. If you're not familiar with weights, get one of the gym regulars to show you. Heavy weights are very dangerous, so please stay away from those grunting gorillas until they are resting between sets. Only then will they notice your loveliness. When they're training, they're working. And when they're working, they're focused. But as you know, a man must breathe. It's a biological fact. Shine your prettiest smile in the direction of his breath.

On ski slopes it is hard to miss single men. In the lift lines they seem to be looking for you. The more often you ride the lifts, the more your chance for conversation. In fact, you could wear your sexy ski clothes and ride the lifts all day!

Stadiums of all kinds are loaded with single, available men. Even though you may not be the athletic type, force yourself to go to baseball, football, and hockey games, tennis matches, golf tournaments, and marathon races. Try anything that deals with sports. It's also healthy for your head. Bowling is close to golf in popularity, so check it out if you want to have plenty of opportunities. You are likely to come up with a prize.

Magazine stands are raging with single male hormones. I have yet to stop by for a paper or magazine and not see several men hovering around auto, mechanic, or provocative mags. You'll find them there on Friday or Saturday nights, especially if they don't have dates. People who are interested in world events or who just like to keep abreast of the latest whatever will always pick up something to read on their way home from work.

You're going to hate this, but financial seminars are occupied with mostly men. Men who want to enrich their lives learning about the stock market, investments, bonds, and so on. And in our poor economy where foreclosures abound, not only will you have your choice of well-wishers, but you might also learn something beneficial for your own future. And that ain't bad.

Don't be embarrassed by singles gatherings. If you don't have success at some of the locales, then check it out. There's certainly no harm in it, and you might come out with a gem in jeans.

Let's not forget *home improvement* stores. Tim Allen is a current television star for a reason. Men definitely have a huge ego about their homes—all men. It's territorial pride. Whether or not they are adept at making improvements isn't an issue. The fact is they *will* try. Their adrenaline surge is fabulously infectious when they succeed at fixing something. You will always find mucho hombres at home improvement stores. I guarantee. The same for lumber yards. There are many manly construction workers buying lumber for their jobs. There are several well-known and successful actresses either married to or dating construction hunks. Talk about a *real man*! Um-hummm . . .

While you're inspecting the merchandise, do not lose sight of the true reason why you want a man in your life. You want a partner; a friend; a good man who will enhance your life; a companion with whom you can grow, create, laugh, love, and have incredible nights of irresistible sex. Keep all of this in mind when your eyes lock with his and your heart flip-flops to the tune of "Please help me, I'm falling!"

THE MALE OF THE SPECIES

Snips and snails, and puppy dogs' tails! That's what little boys are made of!

—ANONYMOUS

Before we talk about dating in general, let's become acquainted with a few qualities in good men. Age has nothing to do with a man's goodness. I've known men at thirty who have experienced all of Job's tragedies and come out winners. I've known other men fifty-five and older who haven't a clue and probably never will. You can't judge a good man by his age, and you can't judge a good man by the amount of crisp new hundred-dollar bills he unrolls. You can, however, consider the following:

He should be emotionally healthy, having learned positive views from life's lessons. He does not blame anyone for his misjudgments or mistakes. In other words, he takes control of his life and responsibility for himself.

He should have strong moral values, conviction, integrity, and a sense of honor; he does the right thing regardless of how tough it seems.

He should be able to endure emotional upheaval (perhaps he already has)—a tragedy, a personal loss, perhaps even a sick or disabled parent or child. Through the ordeal he gains perception, sensitivity, and concern. Without any of life's calamities, his character doesn't have a chance to grow.

He should be above narcissism. I was out to dinner one evening with a want-to-be charmer, but I had the feeling that he was addressing an audience of thousands seated behind me. Every inflection, every turn of the head, every hand gesture, or every glance was choreographed to seduce his public. Beware if he looks in the mirror more than you!

He should be detached from drugs and/or excessive alcohol.

Finally, he should genuinely like women. Some men have a subconscious disdain for women. If your intuition tells you that he does, close the door.

Let's explore other prototypes of certain men you may find:

MR. PARTICULAR

Mr. Particular carries the image of a specific woman in his mind. Terry, a forty-two-year-old Washington, D.C., lobbyist said, "I have always preferred blue-eyed blondes, usually five feet eight inches tall, 126 pounds, in their late twenties or early thirties. I know I'm looking for the perfect woman because every time I go on a date, I get this feeling that she may not measure up. I mean, what if I marry the girl I'm having a relationship with and then later meet my dream woman? I'll begin resenting my wife." Mr. Particular is obviously afraid of commitment, so he devises defense mechanisms to avoid marriage at any cost. He will isolate himself if need be and color or slant a situation to fit his framework.

MR. RUNAROUND

Mr. Runaround loves to date, *period*! He is charming, handsome, inventive, and plans everything down to the appropriate mineral water at dinner. At dinner, each date and outing is perfectly orchestrated—the most divine Italian restaurant with Pavarotti singing in the background, the best wine, the best food, the best ambience, the best of everything—or perhaps it's a wonderful night of jazz under the stars at the Hollywood Bowl complete with great seats, a perfectly prepared basket of food, wine, fruit, cheese, coffee, cognac, and dessert; a blanket if it gets cold; and a pillow for your precious buns. When you return to the car, he plays a CD of the music you just heard.

How appropriate, how prepared, how romantic, how thoughtful. How dangerous to fall in love with Mr. Runaround. He will be so elusive, so controlling, so incapable of committing to you. Let's give him his due. He *is* a great date! He's just not looking for the intimacy of a deep ongoing relationship to nurture. Next!

MR. CONVENIENCE

I know a man who was the Don Juan of Los Angeles, California. He's fiftyish, and until recently his entire life had been dedicated to his art and women. He never wanted marriage for himself. He simply had no desire. Nothing's wrong with that. Each person marches to the beat of a different drummer. That is Mr. Convenience. Oddly, though, things can change. One day, he met

Ann. They worked together on a project. She had a lot of qualities on his wish list. They dated for a while—and then married. A natural harmony has developed, as well as a family. Perhaps it was timing. It often is.

MEN AND AGE

Men's attitudes concerning dating and marriage, in general, do change at various stages. Although it's difficult to generalize, there are certain characteristics you'll find at various ages and stages of development. For example, a man in his late teens and twenties is primarily controlled by his raging hormones—our old friend testosterone. Testosterone gives a male youth a voracious sex drive, unharnessed energy, and ephemeral qualities. Without a clear head and strong convictions, he can easily be led astray. But he can also mature in fine fashion by setting certain goals for himself and seeing them to completion.

Men in their twenties also desire a lot of sexual gratification. And if it doesn't materialize after a few dates, they often move on to another potential conquest. From my interviews, I have discovered that men in their twenties still engage in a diversity of sexual partners, but most of them use condoms.

Also in this age category are some exceptional young men—rare and few—who have decided to settle down with a wife and work toward being a good provider. A woman has a better chance of teaching and shaping a man in this particular age group, because he's still impressionable, ready, willing, and able to be molded with the right words, the right touch, the right care, and the right love. And he's ohhh so willing to let her guide him through whatever stages of sex that she desires. Whether it's playing games, dressing up, or exchanging roles, he's happy to penetrate in the forest, in the ocean, in a plane, or in a tree. Remember, he's still learning. And testosterone's symphony won't often allow him to say no to anything you ask concerning the ol' in-and-out.

Men in their thirties are quite wonderful in another way. They have newly discovered sensibilities. The look of maturity finally arrives and they're usually more accepting of themselves. They're beginning to relax with what God gave them—mentally and physically. Oh yes! They still crave satisfaction just as frequently, but a new hue of growth is added to the horizon—a rich red. According to Phil, thirty-four, an internist and friend of mine, "I was dating an actress who makes karate films and I was crazy about her, to say the least; but I discovered after eight months of dating that she lied often, was insincere and just not the type of woman that I would want to raise my children. I finally got the message that she was money hungry. Now I'm dating a woman with an honest and good heart. Sex with the karate girl was incredible, but sex with my new lady is even better because I know she really loves me."

Men in this age group are usually either getting ready for marriage and a family, or they've been through a divorce. If you happen to date a divorced thirty-something, you need to find out if he learned from the marital experience and its breakup or if he's carrying baggage with "blame" written all over it. So watch his body language carefully when he speaks: Does he appear laid-back most of the time, but prone to sudden profanities when an incapable driver rudely pulls in front of him? Does he act like a poor, vulnerable puppy, or does he confess his mistakes with conviction? If your instinct tells you that this man is consistent, then believe it! Your instinct doesn't lie. Take a moment and really listen.

There are two categories of men who turn forty. I adore the ones who seem to be in touch with themselves—feeling comfortable, satisfied, and glad to be forty for all the wisdom they've acquired. They like themselves. The key is *like*. However, the reverse is also true. Many men at forty look in the mirror and cannot recognize their reflection. Instead of feeling joy and pride, they feel like failures whose time has run out and whose mortality has become self-evident. They evaluate their lives, their jobs, their bodies, their wives and families. Quickly, they try to change everything to mimic their adventurous, fun, and sexy days in high school and college. And you know what that means—a cute, tight-bodied Playmate look-alike. So look out if you have a menopausal male, because he'll need a lot of care, caressing, attention, love, and consideration while going through it. And unfortunately, it may be a few years on the steep face of the Matterhorn.

In a man's desperate attempt to regain his lost youth, he's capable of changing his job, wardrobe, hairstyle, or diet. He may begin an exercise program, drop old habits, take a new lover, or, quite possibly, get a divorce—all to convince himself that he's still a contender. In general, he will race Father Time by challenging his strength, his stamina, and his sex appeal. He simply wants to know if he's still desirable.

On this "proving" ground many men hurt themselves. Harry Bloomingdale reputedly had a cardiac arrest when sharing his masculinity with a girl a fraction of his age. In Tennessee Williams's play, *Cat on a Hot Tin Roof*, the aging Brick drives out to his high school football field one night and tries to jump hurdles just to test his once-great athleticism. He falls and breaks his leg during the drunken escapade. His mind remembers the routine, but his body forgets.

Accepting change is very difficult for these gentlemen. They want desperately to hold on to a certain part of their youth. But it's impossible. And yet, if a man takes exceptional care of himself—a lot of exercise, appropriate sleep, good food, and a positive attitude with a nurturing woman, he can look and feel surprisingly young for quite a while.

Wouldn't it be ideal if your man could move gracefully through each new year with a maturing ease and self-assurance, growing ever more beautiful. Unfortunately, that's asking far too much from the suffering midlife searchers. If the forty-somethings could only understand what a man named Joe Kogel has figured out, they would find peace within themselves: "The worst thing in your life may contain seeds of the best. When you can see crisis as an opportunity, your life becomes not easier, but more satisfying." See, it's attitude all over again.

Now, for the fifties and over: Ted Turner, Clint Eastwood, Sean Connery, Tommy Lee Jones, Warren Beatty, Bob Dole, Charlie Rose, and Jack Kemp are but a few great examples of men who have passed the half-century mark and not only look terrific, but maintain a positive attitude while continuing to work, create, and strive toward their vision. They seem sincerely satisfied with themselves and this stage of their life. If you're so inclined, this is a wonderful age group to date and to marry, if you happen to find one who is not already married.

A man over fifty has done it, seen it, been it, had it, loved it, lost it, felt it, and for better or worse knows what he wants. The good news is that his menopause is over (or it should be). He is much more in tune with the rhythms of life. And when he dates, it's usually a woman with whom he shares a common interest and who is closer to his age. He's not likely to go surfing in Malibu in the dead of winter to prove he's a man. It was said of Jacqueline Kennedy Onassis that she found great happiness with Maurice Templeton, an older gentleman who shared his life with her. He was good to her, helped her with her finances, and was by her side through her decline. A lot can be said of a man who sticks with you! There are so few.

Of course the fifty-somethings and beyond still have fantasies. I hope they always will. Fantasies excite the adrenaline and keep a person invigorated. But do they react to the fantasy? Usually not. They are too wise and comfortable with themselves to waste precious and valuable time chasing an illusion. They want the real thing—to love, to hold, to feel, and to enjoy the different seasons of nature. They like dependability and affection. And much like a woman, they go for substance, stability, and sustenance.

It's only natural to look at and enjoy the vision of a pretty, attractive woman, but these men no longer swing from the trees beating their chest to get a young girl's attention. Tarzan simply prefers sitting in his tree house with his Jane watching the sun rise and set, enjoying a good meal, a good glass of brandy, a good book, a good joke, and good sex from time to time. He's earned his bowl of cherries. He closes his eyes with a smile and a warm feeling of contentment in his heart.

Dating is much more appreciated and never taken for granted by this group of men, partly because they realize that special moments are finite, and partly because they know exactly what pleases them.

DATING—ANXIETY 101

Man is young as long as he can repeat his emotions, woman as long as she can inspire them.

—OSCAR WILDE

No matter what your age, dating is like taking a class in Anxiety 101. And it's important to know that you are dreadfully like other people, men included. Everybody, and I do mean everybody, feels anxious and insecure when they go out on a date, especially a first date. Your sense of inner security has everything to do with your romantic success.

Examine what you really want when you meet a man who appeals to you. A lot of women flirt, tease, and come on to a guy to get him interested, and then reject him. Why? Because she may feel threatened, resentful, and uncertain about being able to fulfill his needs—sexual or otherwise. Fearing physical contact or feeling desperate to have a man in your life will absolutely jump-start anxiety and ruin what could potentially be an exciting romance. Some women flirt by rote, for no reason at all. But, when the man responds —she jumps off because she is not prepared for a relationship.

So if you like men and really want to have *a relationship*, be prepared, be confident, and you will find a man with whom you can share a mutual love. As Katharine Hepburn said, "The trick in life is not getting what you want, it's wanting it after you get it!" To avoid this particular trap, know in advance exactly what you want, lighten up, and open up. And don't make every man you date feel as though he must walk down the aisle with you . . . tonight. You certainly won't be a hit; you're more likely to remain a miss.

Know in your mind that to be a success you don't have to have the face of Venus, the brains of Minerva, the grace of Terpsichore, or the figure of Juno. In other words, you don't have to be a brain surgeon, climb mountains, and wear a G-string. It's much more important to be approachable, to show a man a little encouragement. The right smile from across the room can spark his fire. Or a little flirtatious eye contact now and again will give him something to shoot for.

So it worked! He's walking in your direction. Ahh, he stops and engages you in conversation. Good girl. Now, don't sit there and give him yes and no answers. *Think!* Notice something about his person that you can compliment. Maybe his haircut. Or if he's wearing a suit and you like his tie, then tell him so. Men love it when you compliment their ties. Or maybe you notice the cut of his suit, the style of his shoes, and so forth. Maybe he's wearing a great pair of jeans and a fabulous black leather jacket. Compliment the color or whatever feature you notice first. Fortunately, in jeans, you can be fairly sure of the shape of his legs and his buns, right? Unless they're two sizes too large and he's into the latest fad that hangs rather than fits.

After a while, ask him about himself, but be careful not to get too personal or pry into intimate subjects. If you appear to be curious about his salary or his investments, he'll think you're after a loan rather than his charms. Mark, forty, a financial broker in Los Angeles confided, "I've dated a couple of women who on the first date had the audacity to ask me how much money I made." I find asking such questions supremely tacky. That kind of intimacy is likely to come later if the two of you are serious about one other.

You should never go on a date with a man if you're only interested in his bank account. Life's too short for such hypocrisy. I know several women who married men for their money only, and they're pitifully empty, sad, and lonely inside. They also have dead eyes. But if you happen to fall in love with a man who happens to have a thick wallet, lucky you! And yes, it is just as easy to fall in love with a rich man as it is a poor man. Just be sure it's the *man* you're in love with and *not* the size of his wallet.

The key to engaging the man you want is to find a common ground of interest. If he's reticent and shy, then tell him a bit about yourself. Share your interest —something current that impressed you—maybe a hot new movie, an experimental theater, the latest popular book, a recent sports event, or the newest number one CD. But whatever the topic, keep it light, flirtatious, and friendly.

Always listen in a way that will make him feel relaxed and special. Place all your attention on him when he's talking. Don't dart your eyes around the room muttering, "Yeah," or "Uh-huh," because that's not involved. No matter who the person, with a little subtle investigating you may hit on a subject he likes. Then watch his eyes light up. When you hit a home run, communicating will be fun.

I don't know if you've seen Vice President Al Gore being interviewed on Larry King, but this exceptional talk-show host expertly brought out the intriguing and funny side of Mr. Gore's personality. After watching him blush, laugh, and make fun of himself, you would think the wooden jokes that have been repeated about him are ludicrous. Mr. King has learned to draw out the best from even the most difficult guest, mainly because he is sensitive to nuances of conversation and asks pertinent and interesting questions. In different ways, Barbara Walters, Phil Donahue, and Charlie Rose share the same gift. We could all take lessons from their style. The key is finding out what turns a person on. And you can only do this by listening and paying close attention to the answers along with his body language, then asking the right questions.

During conversation, also remember that guys hate a serious, romantic link too soon. It scares them away. Just be yourself and keep your feminine mystery intact.

Communication is the fertilizer for the flowering of

a relationship. You must let him know your preferences as well. Don't be afraid to communicate your preferences regarding ambience, and activities you enjoy. The place and type of dress needed for the date must be broached before he comes to fetch you. You needn't ask him what you should wear, but you should ask if it's casual or dressy. And there's no harm inquiring about his dress. You must communicate or else one of you will be miserable.

I happen to love surprises, but . . . I make it a point to communicate the type of surprises that turn me on. Once a man understands a variety of things you like, he can please you with unbridled creativity and inventiveness. Otherwise, the surprise could be unpleasant. I want to share one of my unfortunate episodes involving a surprise brunch. For about a year, a fellow actress–girlfriend named Sally wanted me to date her husband's best buddy, Jerry, a very witty and attractive director. We met. He made me laugh and I thoroughly enjoyed his company. He asked me out. I agreed to brunch. It was a beautiful Sunday morning. I took my usual morning run and dressed for what I thought would be a posh hotel brunch—pearls, stockings, high heels—the works.

He arrived in his Land Rover ready for a rendezvous at the beach or the mountains. Anyway, my feminine self hopped into his truck and I told myself to give him a chance. He described a charming restaurant overlooking the beach where we could dine. Well . . . we drove and drove and drove—on the freeways, up the mountains, along the ocean, while I slowly watched brunch turn into lunch. The bright morning light had evolved into the noonday sun before we reached our destination. We parked. He opened my door and we walked up to a closed restaurant. Yes, *closed*! I was tired, starved, frustrated, and angry. He suggested another restaurant down the road. We drove once again, but never did find an open restaurant. I firmly asked him to turn in to the first grocery store we passed. We shopped for takeout food and actually made a quick picnic. Then we drove across the street to a private section of beach, sat down, and gobbled the food. I don't think I said two words to him during the meal or the drive back. Jerry is a wonderful man. It's just that we are not on the same communicative wavelength. Hopefully this experience won't happen to you, because it was dreadfully disappointing.

A good rule in the art of the chase: think of the men that you have been attracted to in the past. Aren't they the ones who like you, but keep you wondering, rather than the ones who call you all the time and are always available? Most people want what they can't get. If a woman is too easy, a man doesn't feel as though he has won a prize. But don't make it too difficult, either. He may pass over you for a woman who acts more interested in him. Be honest, but be reserved. Always hold back a little. In the end, it will pay off. Let him discover your essence as slowly as perfumed petals open on a rose. Discovery is the beauty of a relationship.

During the discovery phase, engage your two feminine forces—teasing and flirting. You need these allies as part of playing and having fun with the love game —lust, love, and romance. But there are two distinctively different types of teasing and flirting: the playful, feminine, and fun kind, which you will find in Scarlett O'Hara from *Gone with the Wind*; or the insincere and frivolous kind depicted in Geena Davis's character from *Thelma and Louise*. You may recall that Thelma became severely intoxicated, then began flirting with, teasing, and rubbing herself all over some country stranger. The more Louise warned her to stop, the more Thelma drank, and the more provocative with the stranger she became, until . . . they walked outside, he pinned her facedown against a truck, ripped off her panties, unzipped his own pants, and took liberties. When you tease the wrong man, you could very well end up in some dark-alley circumstance. Please be careful.

Now take the same erotic, seductive body rubbing, lip licking, finger touching, and toe teasing and turn it toward your true man. *Whooaah, Nelly!* That hot stuff should be for your fella only. Teasing is beyond flirting. Flirting is playing at love, acting a bit coquettish—a twinkling of the eyes, a toss of the hair, a girlish smile and blush, a subtle crossing of the legs, a movement of your body in his direction, or a touching of his arm to feel his muscles. Whereas teasing is a more serious form of foreplay. It's a calculated physical action—a mindset to achieve something. When your stockinged foot rubs his leg under the table, or when your fingers find a bundle of goodies in his trousers while at dinner . . . that's teasing! It's fun and exciting when it's your man that you're teasing.

At dinner, don't play the jealousy bit. It shows insecurity. Just as you hate hearing about his exes, he hates hearing about your past conquests. Instigating jealousy is futile. There's absolutely no point in making him turn pea green with envy. It will only lace the air with negative energy instead of positive fanfare. Besides, a divine seductress does not need her ego massaged in this way. There are other, more direct, and sexually erotic methods for ego inflation.

Also, forget about his *potential*. I know more women who like a guy for what he's going to do, or the job he's going to get, or how much money he's going to make, ad nauseam. *Now* is who and what he is —not tomorrow and not next year. You can only intuit his development. That, too, is like looking into a crystal ball and seeing the future. Hmmm . . . Impossible? One can never tell, but it will be a long, arduous wait until he matures into the man you envision. If, in fact, you are dissatisfied with him at present, don't expect to be satisfied with him in the future. He is what he is!

Like your man for himself. Like him for the manner in which he adds to your life, or find a man who has already developed his potential. You don't need to be nurturing someone else's possibilities; you need to be nurturing your own. Time goes by so quickly. It's all a snapshot . . . snap, snap, snap! One day, you look in the mirror and *say what*? What are all those charming, characteristic tracks of life doing on *my* face? At which time, if your man still hasn't developed into the fantasy of who you think he is, you will not only resent everything he stands for, but you will also hate him for not fulfilling your expectations. Happens every time!

To avoid deceiving yourself, take a good, long look at the whole picture before you start spending your precious time on a man's potential. I was in love with the illusion, once. The lesson cost me my entire savings and a few precious years. Guess what? The man is still full of undeveloped potential. That's when I realized a woman has two choices: either be happy with the man himself, flaws and all, or show yourself to the door . . . *Leave*! Tomorrow is just a state of mind, nothing more.

Now that we know you're in love with the real man and not his potential, let's snap into action. Do you want him to ache with lust? Of course you do! Well, you can dazzle that darling with your sultry voice, simmering glances, an innocent brush or two of your hand over a piece of his clothing, an intoxicating whisper in his ear at dinner, or a stance close enough for him to inhale your perfume . . . always close, but not too close; a slight brush, not a solid touch. It certainly won't be a secret when the hot coals of attraction are forcing both of your energies together. It's in the senses.

You simultaneously see it, smell it, taste it, hear it, and the two of you are craving to touch it. It's hard to hold back, if you catch my drift.

You know in your heart that the man is profoundly physically and sexually interested—wanting to be closer than is humanly possible. So the only thing you need to do is . . . *wait*! Yes, wait. I know you would like to tear his shirt off and devour every inch of his divine flesh, but it's in your best interest not to rush the lust. Delay the inevitable moment. It's not going away, not when so strong a desire and passion are the precursors.

So far, it's been a delicious date with seductive thoughts of kissing, touching, embracing, and slipping into the Sargasso Sea with pieces of his landscape. Why complicate the night? Keep it nice and easy and he will be relieved that you made him wait. It's *you* and no one else he wants. Stir his rich palate of emotion. Never give in too soon or too easily. Orchestrate the level of heat and harmony.

Remember: men always want what they can't have. Get to know him better. His character is just as important as his touch. This brings to mind an unforgettable moment in the Martin Scorcese film *The Age of Innocence* when Daniel Day-Lewis is in a moving carriage with Michelle Pfeiffer. After not having seen her for many months, he takes her gloved hand and holds it as delicately as he would fine porcelain, and with slow suggestive caresses his two fingers begin to open each button, gently peeling back the cloth to undress her vulnerable flesh. With wanton desire, his burning lips kiss her exposed wrist with a soft but consuming passion. Her body shivers. Her searching mouth surrenders in reckless abandon. That one action displays the intense power of lust combined with the truest love. You'll know when he loves you. There's no mistaking it. It's in his eyes, his touch, his actions.

In contrast, there is a scene in *The Godfather* that is more about lust than about love. Remember the early wedding sequence where the bride's (married) brother Sonny made off with one of the bridesmaids? Well, that short scene in the film was much more fully developed and described in Mario Puzo's novel. The scene as written was worthy of several reads—volcanic, to say the least. I highly recommend you get hold of the book and read it yourself.

A word to the wise: if this pure primeval electricity falls upon you, don't fool yourself into believing it's love. It's not! However, if the two of you are available and you really like and respect what each other is capable of giving, then you have a tremendous chance for a loving relationship to blossom.

TO KISS OR NOT TO KISS

A kiss, when all is said, what is it?
. . . a rosy dot
Placed on the "I" in loving; 'tis a secret
Told to the mouth instead of to the ear.
—CYRANO DE BERGERAC

After he brings you home, the next burning question remains—to kiss or not to kiss? At the moment his face nears your lips and your heart jumps into your throat, if the evening has tasted of strawberry parfait and the conversation has had the effervescence of champagne, then absolutely yes! Absolutely, positively yes! But if all is not copacetic and there were a few red lights of warning throughout the course of the evening, then you'd best be prudent. There's not a more intoxicating, romantic, or enduring symbol of love than *the kiss*. So be careful on whom you bestow such sublime enchantment.

I asked several guys to describe the best kisses they've ever had. Collin, a thirty-nine-year-old college professor from Scottsdale, Arizona, gladly responded with: "I don't want to feel like I'm doing all the work. I prefer a meeting of the tongues. But not a tense and insistent tongue that makes me feel as if she hasn't kissed in years. That's the tongue that strikes into my mouth like a cobra. And I don't like mushy or passive kisses."

Jack, forty, a cowboy in Billings, Montana said, "I think a kiss should be soft and slow and very moist, but I don't want to have to wipe my face on her shoulder from all the drooling. I also like it when a girl puts her arms around my neck and touches my face while she's kissing me."

Kevin Costner's character in the film *Bull Durham* deliciously expressed his views on kissing: "I believe in the soul, the cock, the pussy, the small of a woman's back . . . the sweet spot, soft-core pornography . . . and I believe in long, slow, deep, soft wet kisses that last three days!"

Anyone can learn to kiss, whatever their endowment—small lips, big lips, long tongue, short tongue, large teeth, or no teeth. It's all in the attitude and the approach—the feeling behind what you're doing and whom you're doing it with.

As Marlowe's Doctor Faustus said, "Sweet Helen, make me immortal with a kiss. Her lips suck forth my soul; see where it flies!" To be able to suck forth your man's soul and make it fly, begin with a relaxed mind and relaxed jaw. Then with parted lips edging toward his mouth, your laser-beam eyes at half-mast sending silent signals of how much you want his sex, greet his lips ever so gently with a tender hello kiss. After he feels your soft display, open your mouth a little wider, explore his essence—breathe his breath, smell his skin, taste his essence. He may give you his tongue partially. Touch it slightly with yours as though you were sipping a fine brandy for the first time—not too much too soon. To tease is to please.

With slow movements a natural familiarity will slide into rhythm. When he offers a bit more, you give a bit more, until a tango of the tongues ensues. Then with the point of your tongue delicately circle his lips. After he gives you a broader, longer, deeper stroke of his muscle, respond by gently sucking on it a few times. For more titillation, cover your teeth with your lips and carefully bite down on his tongue. Then rhythmically suck on it again with the intention of giving him fellatio. It'll drive him mad. The soft sounds of nibbling, biting, and sucking on his lips from time to time are also erotic.

You can spend hours exploring each other's senses with your lips, breath and tongue. A few sincere moans and groans are extremely sensual. And with grace and direction, your pointed instrument can circle around his teeth. Simply from an erotic and gentle kiss you can learn more about him than he probably knows about himself. Your confidence and creativity will torch his soul if he's a sensual being.

If the kissee does not respond in kind, perhaps it's because he doesn't know how. Maybe he's never experienced a woman who really loved him. Only you can decide if you care enough to show him the way. Some men learn quickly and others need more time. Take it slowly, be patient, and impart your knowledge with loving care. If this is the man who's captured your heart, then he is definitely worth the wait.

A full oral, erotic kiss is exquisitely intimate and can arouse untamable passion. It's akin to intercourse.

The mouth is constructed from similar components as the vagina—membranes, juices, and muscles. So, this masterful game of love play will ignite his unyielding weapon in the direction of your perfume garden. Steal his mouth with your best kiss and you will steal his heart, too.

FOODS FOR LOVE

A good cook is like a sorceress who dispenses happiness.

—ELSA SHIAPARELLI

Do you have enough *juice* in your love? Is your relationship dripping with *moisture* and *succulence*? Does your lover call you *ripe, luscious, mature*? If not, you may want to add the ultimate spice to your life—*aphrodisiacs*.

Just listen to that word—*aphrodisiac*. It conjures up images of the goddess Aphrodite, her nude form rising out of the seashell. We recall the ancient Greeks, teasing their concubines with stems of bursting cherry-red grapes; the Arabs and Egyptian pharaohs swallowing salty seawater to enhance their sexual powers and stamina; the gods themselves imbibing ambrosia, the elixir of love and wild abandon. Speaking of ambrosia, in the South we make a dessert of several mixed fruits, topped off with freshly shredded coconut and maraschino cherries. And once you start eating it, you simply cannot stop. That's probably why it's appropriately called ambrosia, the food of the gods.

Foods, spices, and herbs have been used for centuries by both men and women to stimulate their partners into more passionate and fulfilling lovemaking. In this section, we will take a closer look at some of the more popular aphrodisiacs.

A smart woman knows that the fastest way to a man's heart is through his stomach. But in her zeal to feed her beloved beast, she needs to remember the principle of moderation. Sometimes, in her determination to demonstrate her culinary skills, she is too successful— and her man ends up with a potbelly, love handles, or even a spare tire! A light meal can either be foreplay or afterplay; but it needs to fire a man's lust, not put him to sleep. You want his belly to be happy, yet with room left over for dessert . . . *you*!

The world of food itself is sensual with delicacies that delight the eye and please the mouth. Some of these foods of arousal, for example chocolate, contain a natural substance called phenylethylamine which is thought to be a true aphrodisiac with "love" molecules. This fact is strangely ironic since the act of being in love can cause the body to manufacture its own phenylethylamine. So the one aphrodisiac that lovers truly need is each other's company with a bar of Hershey's for a quick fix. Their closeness causes them to generate their own "love" molecules.

Now let's venture into Mother Nature's cupboard of liquid aphrodisiacs—potions of love. The brilliant advice of Shakespeare reminds us, "It [alcoholic beverage] provokes the desire, but it takes away the performance." There is nothing more gracious than being a charming hostess and offering your man some liquid refreshment for his tired weary throat. But don't offer too much too soon!

Science is not quick to acknowledge the efficacy of aphrodisiacs. Many scientists feel that aphrodisiacs are a placebo—or perhaps a man is deficient in certain nutrients and when these nutrients are replenished, voilà —the long-awaited "whopper"! However, there is one

aphrodisiac that has a confirmed mechanism of action
—the legendary Spanish fly. It is a fluid found in Meloid
beetles, blister beetles. When alarmed, these beetles exude dangerous fluid from their knee joints. When ingested
by humans, Spanish fly acts as a urinary tract irritant
that indirectly stimulates the genitals. The painful burning of the genitals was once considered a sign of lust.
The Marquis de Sade was famous for using Spanish fly
on himself and on those he wished to seduce. Unfortunately, it's a poison so toxic that as little as a tenth
of a milligram can blister and burn the skin and in high
doses it is lethal. So beware of this potent potion of
nature. Pain is definitely not the same as eroticism.

Rumors abound that ginseng, a nutritious herb
from the bark of the yohimbé tree found in Korea, Rus-
sia, and China, not only calms the nervous system, but
also gives a thrust to virility. I know people who swear
that ginseng has straightened many a loose tool. There
are hundreds of foods and herbs that are used around
the world to awaken the sleepyhead. The Japanese believe that raw eel excites and restores the powers of
potency. For sexual warfare medieval women used the
leaves of myrtle soaked in wine. In modern times, aro-
matherapy offers the same enrichment. However, in
place of wine, diluted brandy or natural vegetable glyc-
erin is substituted.

Many Arabs, Europeans, and Chinese advocate the
consumption of eggs, which are rich in proteins, but
also symbolic of fertility. In the Mayan brothels, cacao
beans were choice payment for a night of bliss. Mon-
tezuma, the Aztec emperor, conspicuously consumed
several cups of the cacao beverage before entering his
harem.

The cacao bean has a long, exciting history. It is, of
course, the raw ingredient of chocolate, and was introduced to Europe centuries ago by the explorer Cortés,

perhaps because of its satisfying richness and sensual texture, perhaps because of its love hormone ingredient phenylethylamine. Or perhaps because of a combination of all these factors, chocolate has been a favorite bedroom delicacy for generations.

Another treat reported to have special power is the black truffle, which contains an androgenic substance similar to male hormones. This musky substance is often used in perfumes. Can you imagine why?

Of course the sensual is not strictly earthbound. Aphrodite's emergence from the seashell depicted most famously in Botticelli's *Birth of Venus* reminds us that anything coming from the sea is endowed with her sexual magic and scent—fish, shellfish, turtles, seaweed, caviar, roe, lobster—seawater itself is reminiscent of the salty taste of semen. And what about oysters?

The great lover Casanova was said to have eaten dozens of oysters daily. I'm sure he needed the protein and minerals from the oysters to replenish his own lost sperm. Ah, yes. A healthy man with a healthy appetite and hundreds of women to vouch for it. Oysters have a smooth, moist texture and a delicate aroma that can be very erotic. They go down so easily that they are affectionately dubbed "sliders."

American Indians ate bear and buffalo for strength, but reserved deer for virility. Today, in many health food stores, deer antler is one of the most popular potions. For the red-blooded male, rare beef comes highly recommended as a potent sexual stimulant. Body parts and intestines of certain animals are still traditional tonics. Rhinoceros horns are used in the East as aphrodisiacs.

Other favorite erotic entrées are fruits such as figs, pears, mangoes, peaches, strawberries, burgundy grapes, bananas, kiwis, plums, pomegranates, kumquats, and maraschino cherries.

For the more creative types, watermelon can be titillating, fun. My girlfriend Sandy made a surprise picnic
lunch for her husband, George. It seemed that sex had
become lackadaisical and she wanted to hold a sexual
pep rally. She decided on a secluded field and unfolded
her goodies under a big oak tree. She promptly took
out a book and began reading a seductive poem aloud,
while George pleased his palate. Then came dessert. The
sultry summer day was ideal for Sandy's watermelon
display waiting on ice. As soon as George sliced the
melon, Sandy dug her anxious fingers into its heart. She
slurped a large red clump into her mouth while letting
its sweet divine juice drip down her chin, neck, and fall
over her breast. She took another slice and rubbed it
over her erect nipples, down her belly to her silken
peach panties already moist with dew. She rubbed her
legs with yet another piece and touched her own erection. George was aghast! Taking advantage, she slid her
own large piece into his mouth. He lost himself in her
freedom, while she doused melon juice over his exposed
engorgement. Sandy jump-started their marital intima-
cies, all in a splendidly concocted afternoon.

In choosing to smear on foods and then lick them
off, be innovative. For sex play, you may want to consider whipped cream, honey, peanut butter, fruit pre-
serves, chocolate eclairs, fudge, caramel, butterscotch
sauces, Popsicles, bananas, and any Jell-O substance.
Also just plain water can be the most sensuous experience of all—still, dripping, flowing, running, splashing,
or raining.

For more heated pleasure, you may add a red-hot
sensuous video. *9½ Weeks* is a good choice. Mickey
Rourke and Kim Basinger are at their erotic best while
making an art out of edible delights. To view another
example of "eating sexy," rent *Tom Jones*, starring Al-
bert Finney. In a movie that was famous for sexiness,

the most provocative scene was of Tom sharing a meal with a woman of loose morals. Their delight in the food and in each other was more expressive and erotic than most scenes that show naked couples kissing!

But whatever your preference, the secret to successful food sex is to let improvisation be your guiding light. Who knows, maybe he wants to decorate your anatomy with vanilla ice cream, strawberry cream cheese, or lemon icebox pie, and lick it off . . . slowly. Then again, he may tantalize your nipples or your clitoris with ice cubes!

Talking about the thrill of the chill, you can also rub an ice cube all over his body, over your body, and into your vagina. Several love partners are purchasing penis-testicle molds. They fill the mold with water, freeze it, and then use the design for love play. The ice design becomes the size of an erect penis, at which point the ice can be pushed into the vagina until the inevitable heat melts it down.

The master of all nature is freedom. Let go. Be adventurous. Serve the law of love in play, in all of your multiplicity. Pleasure is the real delight of existence— the secret flame of rapture. Let your wildest fantasies become reality. Who knows, maybe you'll write the definitive book on the power of aphrodisiacs!

Chapter 4

∙ ∙

Acts of Love

The more knowledge is inherent in a thing,
the greater the love. . . . Anyone who imagines
that all fruits ripen at the same time as
the strawberries knows nothing about grapes.
—PARACELSUS

THE SEX ORGANS

The object in life is not to be the best of the best. It's to be the only one who can do what you do!
—JERRY GARCIA

Making love is an art. Before an artist can sail into inspired creativity, she must spend time learning about the physical tools of her art and how to use them. For example, a painter must know how to stretch canvases and mix colors; a musician must know how to handle and care for his instrument; a dancer must take classes and discern elements of music; a gourmet cook must know how to choose and operate cooking utensils as well as how to select delicious foods; a wine connoisseur must study vintages and possess a fine palate, and a love goddess extraordinaire must know herself and every nuance of her man.

All of this knowledge must be in place before you can paint a portrait, perform a sonata, dance a duet, prepare a culinary delight, choose a great wine, or become a magnificent seductress. That is . . . if you aspire to a *superior* level of achievement. To become a magnificent seductress, you must know and understand the tools of your art—the sexual organs. Wholly understanding both sexes allows you to give your lover absolute pleasure.

Too often (perhaps because of ignorance or fear) our own sexual organs are an unknown quantity or, worse—the object of a smutty joke or, much, much worse—an expletive used to express anger or contempt. But you're smarter than most. You read and learn. You understand that the sexual organs are the essential tools with which you will create your masterpiece. To make magic, you will need to know the what, where, and how of his sexual organs as well as your own. Learn all about them, especially how to use them to your—and his—greatest advantage.

Now let's move on to the mechanics and mystery of sexual anatomy. In the early stages of fetal development, a penis forms in the male from the same tissue that develops into a clitoris in the female. Structures or tissues derived from the same tissue are called homologues. The penis is the homologue of the clitoris; the testicles are homologues of the ovaries; and the scrotum is the homologue of the labia majora (outer vaginal lips). Even the male sex hormone, testosterone, is existent in small amounts in every woman, just as men produce a bit of estrogen.

HIS

Let's start with the basics—the penis, which consists of a shaft and a head. Inside the shaft is his urethra (the tube that carries his urine and semen and opens outside his body through a tiny slit in the top of his mushroom head). A man's penis contains no muscle or bone. That's astonishing when you think of how rock hard it can get. It's actually composed of three rods of erectile tissue, each encased in a strong fibrous sheath underneath his thin, delicate skin (which is also expandable and slides up and down); the rods become firm and responsive when stimulated. Erection occurs when feelings of arousal are processed in his brain and relayed through the nervous system straight to his penis. Although we'd like to think that it's the presence of beautiful, wonderful us that's inciting this vertical miracle, in truth, the cause can be constriction from tight pants or even vibrations from riding in a car or truck. When the penis is filled with a lot of pressure as a result of blood buildup, the valves close off to sustain his erection.

An average erect penis is 4 to 6 inches (most are 5⅜ inches). Under 4 inches is short, and over 6 inches is long. Fewer than ten percent of men have penises longer than 6½ inches. The longest penis ever documented was 13 inches! The blue whale penis exceeds those of all Homo sapiens, measuring 10 feet long. Imagine that! No wonder most men claim an extra inch or two for their penis. But remember, it's not the meat; it's the motion! And during lovemaking, you can make a whale of a difference with your skillful hands and mouth.

Also, don't be fooled by the two basic states—flaccid (soft) and erect (hard). The size of a flaccid penis may not necessarily correlate to the size of an erect penis. For example, a small flaccid penis may grow to be enormous when erect. Again, the opposite may be true. It's all individual. Plus, there is absolutely no relation between a man's penis size and other body parts. So stop looking at hands, feet, and noses for clues. The only clue you'll get is when you're hugging. You'll know by the mountain growing on your stomach when you're kissing. Needless to say, that's a *big* clue!

The circumference of, or thickness around, his penis can be narrow like a hot dog, medium like a banana, or wide like a cucumber. Then there's the matter of inclination and shape. It can be straight, curved upward or downward (the way a banana is curved), or narrow at the base and thicker near the top. This particular shape can sometimes be up to three times as wide at the tip as opposed to the base—so the head stands out in comparison, making the man "top-heavy."

Now that you know all about his penis, let's take a look at the scrotum. You're familiar with the sac beneath his penis, right? The one that holds his testicles? His scrotal skin is thin, loose, and stretchable with a thin layer of muscle. When he becomes sexually stimulated, exposed to the cold or physical exercise, the muscles of his scrotum contract, pulling the testicles inside the scrotum closer to his body. I actually think they're sexier when contracted. It enhances the artistic picture of a solid erection and a tight scrotum. It's so dramatic!

The main reason the testicles hang outside the body is that sperm can only be produced at a temperature lower than body temperature. The testicles are responsible for the production of various male hormones, as well as the sperm cells themselves. Most men like to have their balls touched, licked, and massaged. However, many men don't. It may irritate him when you dance with his dynamic duo, so take care!

It's time to move from the general to the specific. The next time you're making love, really observe the fundamentals. In subtle yet important ways each male organ is different from any other. Study its shape, color, texture, skin tone, shadings, veins, ridges. When he's erect, you can actually see a bulging ridge running through the center of his penis. This ridge is the projection of the uretha, which carries semen or urine.

Watch closely as it rises in stages from its dormancy. It also has a pulse you can feel that beats in the same rhythm as his heart. Observe every nuance. Houdini or David Copperfield could never invent anything as miraculous as what your man can do when he decides to change from a limp piece of warm licorice into a pulsating, penetrating piece of steel with the robust roar of a "Lion King"!

Don't just look. Touch! When stroked, it throbs in the tenderness of your hands; and, at an unexpected moment, like a cuttlefish, it will squirt a milky warm liquid in the place you designate.

Don't stop with looking and touching—smell! taste! hear! (Admittedly, penises don't make much noise, but that's no reason for you not to have all your senses working at full throttle to take in information.) Are you worried that your man will resent all this attention being lavished on his penis? No way, José!

A man loves his "objet d'art" more than any other body part. He tends it, fondles it, protects it, talks to it, admires it, pees with it, and takes great pride in it. His penis is a monument to his manhood; the very thing he spends the most time trying to satisfy, even when he's not thinking about it. He gives it endearing nicknames such as: Little Pete, Little Henry, Brutus, the Big Man, the Mighty Sword, King Cobra, Lightning Rod, John Thomas, Big Bad Ben, Red Rooster—take your pick.

So, ladies, you might as well make friends with it, too, and give it the same importance that he does . . . *enjoy his toys.*

YOURS

Women's sex organs are shrouded in much more mystery—not only are they a puzzle to men, but also to many women who know less about their own organs than they do a man's. There are various reasons for this. First, women's organs are less accessible. Men are exposed to other men in locker-room situations after sports play from childhood on, but women, for the most part, are not. A woman can't even see her own genitalia by merely looking down at it the way a man can. In general, women do not buy pornographic material displaying other women's genitalia. So, your lack of basic information is understandable. Face it, womanhood is mystifying even to *women*. And finding that G-spot? Goodness me! We need a road map, a flashlight, a mirror, and literally hands-on exploration and experimentation to locate our own bodily bliss.

Before you spread your legs wide and get acquainted with your sexual self, know that just as each man has a unique penis, you have unique internal and external genitalia. The vulva—your external genitalia —is camouflaged in sexual fleece. The little mound over your pubic bone in Latin is called mons veneris, or "mound of Venus," from the Roman goddess of love. See, your feminine parts are all about love and the quest therefor.

Next, the labia majora extend from the mound of Venus tapering below the vaginal opening. These folds of skin involve nerve endings, oil and sweat glands, and fatty tissue. They also feel sexy when sucked or gently tugged on.

For your information, the labia can have many folds or they can be smooth. One side can be smaller or larger than the other. The labia can look closed or open and vary in color or odor during sexual arousal. Also, the inner lips (labia minora) can fit inside the outer ones, or they can protrude. Whatever design God gave you, their ability to receive pleasure is infinite.

Now, try squatting over a mirror to glimpse your labia minora flesh—pink, glistening with moisture, and delicately appearing devoid of skin. Your lips extend from directly above the clitoral head to the vaginal opening. These matching folds of hairless skin are not only lacking fatty tissue, but they also have more nerve endings than their outer sisters, making them ultrasensitive. So take care to treat them with gentleness. The color varies from pink or red to purple or black. All these colors are perfectly normal and when you become aroused and excited, the color may change to their formal sex color which is a bright red. Think about it! Everything changes when you become sexually activated.

Let's talk about the female penis, aka the clitoris, which (you remember) develops from the same tissue as the penis and has a similar response. Unlike the penis, it doesn't have a hole or urethra running through it. During my interviews, a number of women were shocked to find out that their clitoris did not expel urine. I'm talking about ladies of all ages. For those of you who want the truth: your urinary opening (urethral meatus) is about 1½ centimeters or ½ inch *below* your clitoris.

Your clitoris is located just below the top where the lips meet. It has a tiny glans and a little hood or foreskin called the prepuce, which is a body of loose tissue. Most of it is inside and not visible. Maybe that explains why most men don't know how to find your clitoris. Either they don't know female anatomy at all, or perhaps they're not interested enough to find out, in which case, you may want to subtly take his finger and place it on your sensitive spot. Show him how to touch the delicate delight by massaging it at your heartbeat rhythm or whatever stimulation you prefer. Keep this thought in mind: direct stimulation on the open love bud is not only uncomfortable, it can also be painful.

When you push your hood upward, you'll see what I am referring to as your love bud. It's that pink root jutting out that's comparable to a tiny button or green pea. That's your clitoris, the most sensitive part of your entire genitalia. It's filled with hundreds of nerve endings. Like a man's penis, it swells when stimulated and becomes firm and responsive. What was Freud's hypothesis? That women have penis envy? Please . . . we have an awesome little pink bud that only receives pleasure and will *never* know performance anxiety.

Located just below the urethral meatus is the entrance (introitus) to the largest tube in your female genitalia—the vagina. It's three to four inches long, flexible, and made of folded muscle. The inside walls are covered with mucus membrane. In fact, the texture, warmth, and wetness of the vagina are similar to that of the mouth, which may be one of the triggering reasons why a sexy French kiss can cause an immediate erection from either sex. French-kissing is the bridge between our mouth and genitalia. You can also French-kiss the genitalia, but we will discuss that topic later.

During arousal, your vaginal walls lubricate, producing a slippery liquid that helps guide and accommodate any size hose for the watering of your lush landscape. If you want to look at your fertile land, I strongly recommend buying a speculum. You can buy a plastic one for about three dollars and have entrance to the gates of heaven.

What's next? The cervix—Latin for "neck." Your cervix is connected to and protrudes into the innermost end of the vagina. Just an aside, but during intercourse, providing your man's endowment is praiseworthy, he can feel your cervix and he will know with your unsolicited screams that Elvis has entered the building! Obviously this does not feel good!

There's a little hole in the center of the cervix called an *os*, which means "mouth" in Latin. Your menstrual flow is like Dorothy journeying to the Emerald City, passing from the uterus to the vagina through the os. The os is the gateway either into or out of the uterus. It's also what your man's sperm must swim through (from the vagina into the uterus) in its race to find your egg.

Picture a juicy ripe pear—turned upside down—wide at the top and tapering at the bottom with the stem hanging downward. That's your uterus or womb.

It's a hollow organ about three inches long and two inches wide that will expand to fit a newborn.

All right, we've discussed vagina, cervix, and uterus. Next in line and adjacent to your luscious red womb are two white ovaries (each about the size of a grape), which produce eggs and sex hormones. Each ovary contains about two hundred thousand immature eggs, and each egg is encased in a thin tissue called a follicle.

Your fallopian tubes are the horns of the uterus. Each attaches at one end to the top of the uterus, with their other end hanging near the ovary. When your ovaries release an egg it must travel through one of the fallopian tubes to reach the uterus. When that occurs, the stage is set for conception. When your man shoots his sperm into your vagina, some sperm goes through the os into the uterus. You can feel this warm glow of love caressing all of your internal genitals. However, it takes at least fifteen minutes for this lovin' feelin' to occur after ejaculation.

BOTH OF YOU

The most powerful sex organ which the two of you share is the brain, the place where you experience arousal, emotional foreplay, and the acme of love-making—orgasm. It produces thoughts and fantasies and helps enable you to achieve orgasmic release. We usually only orgasm in a state of fantasy—a state of virtual reality within our own brains, a belief in the fantasy so powerful that we step out of our ordinary world and enter into the orgasmic world of fantasy. Although it's possible to orgasm using fantasy alone, it is rare. Even Masters and Johnson did not find one person in five hundred cases who could achieve this feat, but they believed it to be true.

The brain orchestrates our whole sex program,

producing endorphins and enkephalins, which cause the ovaries and testes to produce hormones. They also cause the entire sex cycle. So you see, you can control the quality of your sex life by properly programming your brain. It's your call. You can have the will to be mighty, to be divine, to have any orgasm you choose—minor, major, or volcanic.

Speaking of hormones, generally women who produce high levels of the male hormone testosterone are more sexually active or wish to be. They may enjoy sex more than their sisters who produce a normal amount. Certain women who produce ten times more testosterone than other women tend to do most of the riding, positioning, and coming during amorous adventures. The body produces its highest levels of testosterone at the middle of your menstrual cycle, which explains why women become so disturbingly beautiful at that time.

Here's a little secret: when you ovulate, and your corpus luteum (an encasement on the ovary) breaks, it not only discharges a ripe egg; it also discharges more testosterone and also pheromones (the sexual organic molecule that exudes from your skin revealing to males that you're fertile). The testosterone makes us become more sexy; it is a compelling aphrodisiac. The pheromones attract men to you as a female deer attracts lusty bucks when she drops her scent of musk along the fertile trail.

For rhapsodic lovemaking, your brain and sexual organs must work in unison. But start slow. Employ all of your talents and then some. As the gorgeous Brad Pitt said, "Only you know what you got in you!" To teach your man to be a hot lover, you will need to slow him down by your example. Begin with the art of arousal and bathe yourselves in foreplay.

THE ART OF AROUSAL

As long as you know that most men are like children, you know everything!

—COCO CHANEL

Arousal is a game you play with your brain. Although some might consider arousal to be synonymous with foreplay, foreplay ends with intercourse, while arousal can be a continuous state of mind. Don't be afraid to stimulate your mind, to challenge yourself, and to knock Mr. Gorgeous unconscious!

What really feels good to you? What makes your eyes shine and your clitoris chime? What makes your mouth water and sugar walls glisten with nectar? What shameful sounds alert your ears? What lubricates your brain? You don't have to tell anyone. It can be your secret.

Wouldn't it be wonderful if your man knew exactly what buttons to push to keep you perpetually aroused? Realistically, no one can push all the right buttons all the time. Our sexual energy is like the tide. Sometimes it's in, sometimes it's out.

Let's imagine that you're with the perfect lover. Benevolently speaking, it's not fair to put the absolute burden of sexual arousal on his shoulders every time. Sometimes you need to take responsibility for arousing him and yourself. We asked for equality. We certainly have it in this arena. Coming to your lovemaking sessions already turned on is a supreme aphrodisiac for him—much better than banana cream pie.

How can you do it? Take a tip from my friend Mary Ann, a thirty-three-year-old copywriter from Chicago, Illinois, who confides, "I had such hang-ups about my body, about receiving an orgasm, about pleasing a man, until I turned thirty-three years old. For my birthday I took a trip to Big Sur, California, alone. I had an unforgettable experience on the patio of my Ventanna Inn suite listening to the music of Frank Sinatra while the sun penetrated my naked body. Breathing in the natural smells of my surroundings, I unconsciously began touching my own personal natural surroundings—my thighs, breasts, face, and hair. While exploring my womanhood in front of God, I imagined that my fingers were "his"—the man of my dreams—caressing every area of my body in rhythm with the music. Before I knew it, I had goose bumps from head to toe, then tiny spasms. I thought my brain was contracting or hallucinating. The world disappeared for a brief moment. Without warning, a flood of warm wet liquid ran down my thigh. I leaned over the balcony and let loose a yell that would have beckoned Tarzan himself."

The bottom line is, if your man does not arouse you to the point of surrender, do it yourself! If you arrive at that wonderful place, what difference does it make who gets the credit?

Just as an actor prepares for a role, you can prepare for lovemaking by doing things to keep your erotic mind fueled. Remember to treat your libido as a living thing to be nourished and nurtured. Don't neglect it. It's sure to dry and die like a plant that you forgot to water. (Don't you just *hate* it when that happens?) But the good news is: while your plants can die from too much water, your libido only grows stronger and healthier with more encouragement. And you stay younger longer, because the testosterone, pheromones, endorphins, enkephalins, et cetera, generated at that time are exactly the same organic molecules that help rejuvenate your beautiful body. That's a fact!

Now that your motor is humming, what are you going to do for his? Remember that arousal can be inspired by sights, sounds, words, smells, touch—the power of suggestion—anything. And you don't have to look too far to find sources of inspiration. It's not for nothin' that million-dollar industries keep us interminably aroused. We love it. We feed off it. *Stimulate! Stimulate! Stimulate!*

Romantic novels written for women jump off the bookstore shelves. Magazines for men continue to grow in popularity. How different can one woman look from another? Every month they keep finding new interpretations and men ride with the tide. Different is exciting. Different is enticing. But you may ask: how do I keep his aroused energy focused on me?

Since you are the gatekeeper of your jewels, you can—in all propriety—promote an incident in public that will leave him with wide-eyed fascination. Actually, anywhere you sense the tactile tigress taking over, just go for it! You only live once, but check it out first, and do be careful.

Here's an idea. If you're sitting opposite your lover in a restaurant, take your stockinged foot and massage his crotch with your toes; or if you're sitting side by side, let your fingers talk to "Lucky Chuckie" under the table or take your man's hand and put it on your wet tulip. The presence of other people in the restaurant and the danger of discovery will add more than a dash of spice to the proceedings.

For sheer provocation, wear a bra with the nipples cut out. This can lead to arousal for both of you—the feel of the fabric rubbing against your erect nipples will keep you perpetually stimulated while the sight of their protrusion should have a salubrious effect on him.

Throughout the evening, consider bending over to give him a glimpse of your cleavage. If you don't have ample cleavage, buy a Wonder Bra. They're great. Or cross and uncross your legs to let Adonis peek up your thighs. I wouldn't suggest playing the room. Pick your moments. But always be a lady who gives her gentleman a few private diversions. After all, seduction is about anticipation. He needs to look forward to what lies ahead. Or didn't you know that anticipation is extremely arousing? *Anticipation* is the key that unlocks the door of desire. So make him wait!

Flirt! Flirting is intriguing when done with sincerity and charm. Always flirt with the man you love. It keeps the embers stoked. If he has encyclopedic knowledge, stare deep into his eyes with genuine admiration. A knowledgeable gent certainly gives my libido a wake-up call. If he's working on an interesting project, ask him all about it. Let him talk while you listen with adoration. He'll feel a mounting sense of well-being and think he's discovered gold, which he has—you.

Make him feel that whatever realm he's chosen, you are impressed. He's the basis of the earth's core. Be sincere. Be perceptive. Be sensitive. Maybe you have something he can fix. Or a project he can help you finish. Allow him to be manly. That masculine specimen will defend you, protect you, and hold you forever dear in his protective, strong hands.

Also, if you have a flair for humor and know a few provocatively funny jokes or stories, tell him. Remember to keep them amusing, not crude. You don't want to sound like one of the boys in the locker room. Use your humor with aplomb and panache. It will always be one of your greatest allies. There's nothing better than a hearty laugh from the gut to open up a fella. When a man is happy, stimulated, and in love, he will bring you the Holy Grail. Keep it light! Keep it fun!

What about sounds? Is there a singer or a song that turns him on? Find out! You *need* to know these things. Aural foreplay enhances anticipation. Call him at work or leave a message on his machine using sexual double entendres. Whisper a fantasy in his ear, preferably one that excites both of you. He'll get the picture.

Most men love to read erotica. So do most women, for that matter. Only our choices are a bit dissimilar. Give him something artistic, yet suggestive, as a gift or let him "accidentally" come across some of your erotic spirituality and encourage him to thumb through it.

I can't begin to tell you how alluring soft, silky fabrics are to a man's touch. Why do you think lingerie is a billion-dollar business? It's the feel of the fabric against your femininity. Wear them often and position your anatomy in ways that entice his fingers to wander into your wanton zones.

Nonchalantly, ask him to feel the silkiness of your satin blouse, the softness of your cashmere sweater, or the texture of the fine cotton, crepe, rayon, jersey, acetate, or other slinky materials you happen to be wearing at the time. Whatever fabric you choose, as long as it's soft and sensual, it will increase his desire.

If you have no objections, let him run his fingers through your hair. Men love the smell and feel of a woman's clean hair. It's intoxicating to them. Try not to be too concerned about your hairdo, but more concerned for his enjoyment. Now, if you're dashing to the theater, concert, or a sophisticated dinner, that's a different matter. I'm sure he can wait, if you charmingly communicate.

About smells: why do you think we spend so much money and time on perfumes, scented powders, and body lotions? For ourselves? Of course! But also, for our man. I love it when my man inhales the fragrance of my body, whether the clean smell of soap straight from a shower or my tried and true perfume. A suggestion: if your fella responds strongly to a certain fragrance, make a mental note. And when you see him again, wear it. Smell is a central part of arousal and seduction.

Another endearing and inviting smell is the aroma of succulent food cooking in your kitchen. As he walks through your door, the smell of cooking food will seduce his stomach and send his senses to fond memories. My grandmother (who was the best cook in New Orleans) repeatedly said, "The best way to a man's heart is through his stomach!" (I know my grandmother's not the only or even the first one to say it. These sayings become proverbial because they are true.) The hunger for good-tasting, fresh food is another kind of sexy desire. Of course, there are many other feminine wiles, but Grandma's way is tried and true, provided you're a *good* cook. If you're not, beguile him with your other specialties.

Before we withdraw from the smell sense, I'll leave you with the biggest turn-on of all—pheromones—the musky scent which emanates from your vagina and his scrotal skin at certain times. In other words, your natural juices. (These pheromones are different from the ones mentioned above.) When he inhales your pheromones, his gears shift from first to fifth in milliseconds. Presto . . . an erection! It's also a signal that you're turned on, too, and knowing *that* is even more exciting to him than your perfume. It's the domino effect! He gets delirious because you're enthusiastic. Let him savor the scent. You know how testosterone loves estrogen.

Okay, now that you're both aroused, let's experience a potent one-two—emotional as well as tangible foreplay. The necessary stimulation you so deservedly crave before intercourse. And if everything goes well, orgasms for everyone.

FOREPLAY

Don't ever let me catch you singing like that again, without enthusiasm. You're nothing if you aren't excited by what you are doing.
—FRANK SINATRA TO HIS SON, FRANK, JR.

Foreplay is a delicious and exciting activity, usually (but not always) precedent to intercourse. Before we get too involved with the details of how, I want to remind you that engaging in foreplay does not oblige you to conclude with intercourse. You still have the right to stop and say no. I think it's also important to remind you that activities involved in foreplay that don't conclude with intercourse can still result in the transmission of serious illness. I don't want to spoil your fun, but I do want you to be around to enjoy life and your dream man for many years to come, so please heed my warning.

Although matters of sex should always be fun, there is a certain amount of responsibility that never should be abdicated, such as the intimate discussion of sexually transmitted diseases (STDs). Taking appropriate precautions (condoms and regular testing for STDs) is a necessary part of responsible lovemaking. It's wise to have this delicate conversation before you enter into foreplay. Of course, I know you will broach the topic with considerable tact and charm, right? Then exchange proof that both of you are healthy. If he will not go along with the program, he's a cad, he's definitely not living in the real world . . . drop him!

Onward with foreplay. You may be under the impression that men don't need or don't like foreplay. *Wrong!!* During my interviews, I asked the question, "Would you like to be sexually pampered by the woman you love?" Answer: "Oh yeah! Why not? Except I'd have to trust her first, and feel comfortable!"

Ladies, it's time to call forth your consummate womanly wiles—knowledge, imagination, skills, erotic paraphernalia, and other inventive resources. You don't want to be a memory, unless of course it's the kind of memory that Travis Tritt pines over in a song—*the one he can't forget!* Yes, you want to be the woman he will die for, the woman he will never leave, the woman he can't get out of his mind and the slightest thought of whom brings on a "grand erection." To be this woman, you need yet another ally—foreplay—the skill of feel.

Remember that his ability and desire to enjoy foreplay are no less than yours. Be gentle but purposeful. If you've come this far, begin to assess his shape through his clothes to give scope to the preparation of your masterpiece. With your sensitivity and acute awareness, every ounce of his body will be in full cooperation. As you slide your fingertips over his pectorals, feel *his* erect nipples. How naturally his body responds to your touch! Slowly continue to run your fingertips up and down the length of his anatomy. Take your time. Give him a sense of security. Now, use your hands to squeeze sections of his flesh a bit more firmly. At this point, he should be comfortable enough for you to proceed with the complete undressing.

Undress your man with finesse. After you fondle and caress him through his clothes, after he accepts your pre-massage, it's time for more serious and meaningful stimulation.

While you're kissing his lips and massaging the front of his chest, you could begin to unbutton the front of his shirt or, if it's a T-shirt, with your sensitive, nimble fingers slip it over his head. It's not imperative to begin at the top, especially for a man. He may think you're never heading for the gold. And that's precisely the root of his excitement. The *wait*! The *tease*! The *anticipation*! As you open his shirt, make a trail of kisses over all exposed areas. If he has a hairy chest, nuzzle your face in it, smell it, play with it. If his chest is bare, kiss and lick his smooth skin. Whatever he's got, enjoy.

The key to undressing yourself in front of him or undressing him is: take your time with each item of clothing. As you remove each part of his clothing, make love to that uncovered part. In undressing him slowly, you're showing him how you want him to undress you; now it's up to you whether you leave parts of his clothing on or undress him completely. Remember: different moods and surroundings dictate different actions. Act accordingly.

Ahh, so you've decided to undress him completely! Good! Now that he's naked, you can begin to paint his picture. Think of him as the canvas and yourself as the brush and paint combined. Use your exquisitely sensitive fingertips and far-reaching toes to trace a design. Bring your lips and tongue into play to add color and depth. Nuzzle some of those hard-to-reach crevices with your nose and eyelashes. Cover large areas with your soft breasts and hard nipples. Let your silky hair brush all over him. Use every inch of yourself to caress every inch of him. His entire body is an erogenous zone waiting and longing for the immortal touch that only you can bestow.

Your artistry and patience should inspire him to reciprocate in kind. In fact, don't be surprised if he's eager to do so. And then you can fly to Never Never Land on Aladdin's magic carpet—*together*. Moreover, after you please him completely, he'll be the clay for your Rodin. He'll fantasize, hope, and dream for an encore of celebration. In the interim, I'm sure he'll do whatever is humanly possible to make you happy both in bed and out.

Since every man has a different libido, the road to foreplay has no rules—no right or wrong. The guide to your inamorato's erogenous zones lies dormant—waiting anxiously for you to step up to the podium to commence the inauguration. My, my, what power you have. But never forget: you're only as powerful as your sensitivities and acute awareness. Without awareness, your intelligence and artistry are wasted. Your tango can be smooth as silk or rough as burlap. It's your assignment to discover through grace and subtlety exactly what areas delight him most. What touch—how light or firm, where and when he feels comfortable being stroked. His sounds, body movement, and hands will guide you. Pay close attention!

He will have places of pleasure and responses that no other man has. And when you locate the precise place, keep it your secret. If you talk about it or tell anybody, you will lose your magic. Magic cannot survive mistrust.

Don't be impatient. Exactitude rarely happens on the first take. Opening up is a slow and somewhat arduous process, especially for a man. Nonetheless, you might get lucky. Make experimenting on his bodily reactions your life's mission. Finding his turn-ons could be a joy. One day it might be one thing, another day, something else. Since turnabout's fair play, allow him to explore your turn-ons.

Always remember that the *brain* is the engine that drives all erogenous zones. Your allure must run deeper than your killer looks. To really turn him on you must first relax his mind. Expel his negativity and anxiety-ridden thoughts. Instill fun, positive musings such as exchanging provocatively humorous experiences that you've both had, heard, or read. Stimulate his senses with photos, videos, music, or a striptease . . . *anything* enticing. Just free his mind!

Indulge his whims with a bit of role-playing—act out a fantasy. But make sure it's fun for you, too. Project yourself into an imaginary situation, dress the part, and act out the role. Ideally, plan ahead so he can anticipate. Eat light. Be spanking clean. Set the desired mood. Take the phone off the hook and hide the beeper. Use pillows, silk scarves, oils, lotions, incense, sexy foods for sex play; inspire aural foreplay with tempting naughty talk. Take your time and relax with a glass of champagne, wine, juice, or whatever you prefer. The key is to let go of inhibitions. Sometimes role-playing can free both partners' inhibitions.

ROLES

You can be a cheerleader and he the football hero. *Encourage him!* You can be a slave girl and he can be your lord and master. *Please him!* You can be the femme fatale and he can be the innocent farm boy you're initiating into the mysteries of sex. *Seduce him!* He can be the teacher and you can be the little girl who's getting a spanking. An erotic spanking with the right words, the right pressure, the right hand, the right place on your buttocks while you're lying over his lap with your panties partly down, can release a lot of juices. He'll probably tell you how bad you've been while he makes you even badder. Talk about libidinous!

Now that you've opened the door to your imagination, keep exploring that territory. You play the lovely Guinevere who is rescued by the handsome knight Sir Lancelot. *Show your gratitude!* He is the powerful Viking, Erik the Red, and you are his captive. Struggle for a while, then *surrender unconditionally*. Another time, switch roles. You are Captain Hook, the most feared pirate in the South Seas, and you've captured both his ship and his men. Command him to surrender all of his weapons. Tie him to the mast and blindfold him. If he so much as whimpers while you undress him, simultaneously tickle his naked body with a feather and spank his bottom. Maybe with more than your hand. And if he refuses to submit, threaten to throw him overboard, where the sharks will have a banquet with his delicacies. He's your prisoner—do as you will!

Some men really like this type of sport. Ali, a thirty-four-year-old lawyer said, "I love playing the submissive role with my wife, Tina. She dresses in fishnet stockings, a bustier, and six-inch black leather heels. She wears a choker, a mask, and sometimes carries a whip or a feather. She does things to my body that excite me to the point where I get so turned on that I feel silly. She never laughs. She just continues my fantasy. That's why I love her so much. The following week, I'm the party in control and command her to masturbate herself while I watch. Afterwards, I use a few toys and vibrators to excite her to multiple orgasms."

Silly-for-love is not a bad place for anyone to be. But never do anything that makes you feel bad or uncomfortable. Lovers must have fun in their own way, their own style.

Different men have different styles of expressing their erotic side. Some men revel in submission, some men rejoice in domination, some men relish both. There are men who handle women, handle wild horses, and handle life with a certain savage but tender and romantic flair. The classic American lover. But whatever his deepest desires, you won't know until you investigate his inner soul.

MORE MALE ROLES

Playboy, TV anchorman, Chippendale dancer, hair-dresser, famous athlete, psychiatrist, truck driver, sultan, gynecologist, politician, movie star, gigolo, prisoner, Mafia don, traveling salesman, starving artist, cowboy, porno movie producer, rich sugar daddy, pizza delivery boy, rock star, surfer, serious musician, big-game hunter, policeman, stranger, Batman, Dracula, Don Juan, Valentino.

MORE FEMALE ROLES

Lawyer, nun, model, movie star, airline stewardess, librarian, housewife, debutante, sex therapist, jungle queen, groupie, prison guard, princess, professor, harem dancing girl, stripper, tax collector, mechanic, waitress, real estate broker, singer, interviewer, rich socialite, best friend's girl, carhop, judge, cowgirl, Southern belle, farmer's daughter, saleswoman, dentist, highly paid lady of the night.

Imagination is such a dynamic tool for great sex. My friend Katie, a thirty-year-old real estate broker who's married with two children, knows how to make good use of her imagination. "After twelve years of marriage, my husband, Don, and I still make love at least three times a week or more. I wear sexy lingerie and costumes that I put together for his amusement—crotchless panties, pasties on my nipples, fishnet body suits, a nurse's uniform, a school girl's uniform with a black garter belt and stockings underneath and high heels or boots, whatever mood strikes me at the time. I keep things exciting, not only for Don; being sexually aggressive and playing different roles stimulates me, too. Sometimes I wear a particularly sexy dress when we go out to dinner or a party. During the entire evening, I flirt and tease, but I never touch him. I just appear as if I'm about to and it makes him really hot. By the time we get home, I'm ready to devour him. Kneeling on the floor of the kitchen, I unzip his pants and perform oral sex."

Katie and her husband have learned the important lesson that anything is possible in an atmosphere of trust and deep, deep caring. They indulge each other's fantasies in a fun-loving environment while reaping rich rewards.

USE YOUR HANDS

Now both of you are engaged in the process, you're both aroused, both willin', wantin', and waitin' with anticipation. At this point, use everything available to you. You can't find enough ways to use your hands in the art of making him feel good. Mae West certainly used her tactile assets. Take the last scene in her movie *She Done Him Wrong*. Cary Grant (who turned out to be an undercover cop) produced a pair of handcuffs by which he intended to take Mae into custody. She looked at him dubiously and protested, "I ain't never worn a pair of them things." Cary responded knowingly, "A lot of men might have been safer if you had!" From the glint in his eye, I don't doubt that Mae's mouth and fingers strummed a few bars on Cary's instrument. Hmmmmm, hmmmmm, that's a very sexy woman.

Like Mae West, after you've had your expert hands all over his anatomy, he'll be in seventh heaven. If you're sensitive, imaginative, and a bit courageous, he'll consider you and your hands "dangerous." The sexy side of dangerous—butterflies in the stomach, a quickened heartbeat, a juicy mouth, flushed cheeks, can't eat, can't sleep. And does your main man deserve anything less than magic? I think not.

Speaking of hands, who can forget that wonderful scene in the movie *Ghost* where Demi Moore is work-

ing at the pottery wheel? I could see strength
expression flow from her hands while she dug
worked the wet clay. In fact, as Patrick Swayze looke
on in admiration of this sensual and artistic feat, his
hands couldn't resist joining hers at the wheel. Their
"touch" was exquisite to behold. The climax came
when both pairs of hands moved simultaneously, creating a phenomenon of seductive art. Suffice it to say,
seductive art is what you will be creating with your
objet d'art—your man!

REAL ROLES
To love deeply takes a lot of courage and guts—a lot
of patience, nurturing, and reassuring, but the rewards
are great. Are you game? If so, you can gain access to
his cache by choosing a sensitive moment to communicate the following: that you will not think him unmanly
or weak if he lets you take sexual control sometimes;
that he needs to forget all of his preconceived ideas
about who's supposed to be dominant and who's supposed to be submissive; that he does not have to perform on any level; that lovemaking is not tit for tat;
and that it's not about one person controlling every sexual session. It is about *give-and-take—control and surrender*—for both parties.

Your soldier may be prone to hide his submissive
side. That leaves it up to you to change his thinking
with your skillful processing orientation. To surrender,
a man might fear losing his erection and the humiliation
that follows. Reassure him that it's not a contest—keeping his erection is not vital. You're simply cohorts sharing responsibility; advancing the art of lovemaking in a
collaborative process. In fact, at times it's more provocative when he allows *you* to become his fantasy
femme fatale.

Women have tremendous power to be life giving

or life threatening. Lea, a twenty-six-year-old beautiful blonde from Youngstown, Ohio, gets upset when her man is not erect. She said it makes her feel undesirable. Not only is she expecting the impossible, she's also putting unimagined pressure on herself and her fella. It's foolish and insecure to think such thoughts. A man is a human being, not an automaton. He can't be expected to rise on command. In this case, as in many others, the best lubrication and stimulation is still . . . communication!

Take a chance on being the innovator who dares to take your man on the voyage of his lifetime. To be able to get what you want out of lovemaking—kissing, foreplay, orgasm, romance coupled with hot interludes, you need to make love to his body the way you would like him to make love to your body. Show him slowly while expressing, "Does this feel good? I love it when you do this to me . . ." A man will not be able to give you what you need and want if you don't know what you need and want. After you have learned to satisfy your own body, kindly show him by example. No matter how much you wish it to be so, he's not a mind reader, and maybe not as quick as you. Just cut him a little slack. If he's a good one, he's certainly worth it.

Please don't get frustrated if it doesn't happen in one night. It generally takes a few sessions before he finds the right rhythm to draw pleasure from your treasure. Eventually, he *will* get the whole movie and voilà—your phantom lover in the flesh. So tell Tarzan to move over and let Sheena swing on the vines for a while.

Once aware that surrendering is truly sexy, he will give you his weaponry any time, any place. If you doubt me, rent the movie *Desirée* and pay particular attention to the last scene when Marlon Brando, playing Napoléon, surrenders his sword to Jean Simmons, who plays

Desirée—his first love. It is a magic moment. The amazing thing is that both characters emerge from that scene stronger than they were when it began. There are no losers in love. The experience itself is pleasing to a woman.

The main benefit of initiating and leading sex play is you get what you want. Being in control allows you to choose the place, set the pace, tempo, and most important . . . create the right mood to discover and draw out hidden passions. With his body in your hands and at your command, you can make foreplay more sensual and last as long as you desire. Of course, this can only work if you have already earned and *deserved*, not merely *demanded*, his trust.

Go slowly and take your time; feel his anatomy. Let your fingers act as sensors exploring the uncharted territory of his pleasure. Investigate the mysterious regions of his response—what areas and what kind of pressure make him shiver or sigh or moan?

When you've found his bliss, weave in and out, circle around. *Tease* until he's breathless—intoxicated. Then delicately and purposefully use those educated fingers to guide him safely into the quiet glades of Eden, where delirium and emancipation grow with the most incredible foreplay and orgasm he has ever had!

Keep remembering the nonpareil lover who appears to you when you're "petting the pony." He walks through your door or stands at the foot of your bed, drawing you to him like the magnet he is. Unquestioningly, you surrender your whole being to a current of engaging orgasms. After he's drained every last droplet of dew from your orchid, your heart and soul, branch and root belong to him as you lie in his arms perfectly spent.

You see, you do to your man exactly as your ideal sex mate does to you—more or less. Need I say more?

Carry on: treat his entire body as the erogenous zone it is. This kind of communicative lovemaking is more feeling and exploratory than vocal. He might be vocal in expressing his release, but your seductive voice will come later during intercourse. For now, go very, very slowly. Titillate, tantalize, and thrill.

KISSES

We discussed kissing earlier, but now that we're discussing a more intense relationship, here are a few more reminders about kissing. First, as I've stated before, relax your jaw. Since the muscles of the lips are connected to the jaw, when you relax your jaw, the lips relax. Your kiss must be tender, delicate, and with controlled passion, but passion nonetheless. Always kiss gently at first. Cushion your lips against your teeth, so as not to jar or take him out of the moment. He needn't feel your teeth, just your soft, gentle, hungry lips. (A man hates to feel teeth either when you're kissing his lips or his penis.) Also, if you kiss him with tension in your lips, he can't properly relax. He takes his cue from you, remember. And relaxation is the key to enjoyment.

Don't stick your tongue into his mouth before he can taste your lips. After he feels comfortable and wants more, you can gently but firmly rub the tip of your tongue over the front and back of both rows of his teeth. Then delicately suck on his lips. Keep it sensual. No quick movements. (Some men like this, others don't. You be the judge.)

If he gives you his tongue, that means he has accepted you, and his sexual temperature is on the rise, if not risen. But don't let his encouragement rush you. Stay with sensual, tender, and exploring kisses. While you're exploring his lips and mouth with your tongue, keep it pointed, rather than broad and flat. And don't suffocate him by keeping your tongue deep in his throat. You don't have to try to be sensual . . . *you are sensual*—you're a woman!

When his mouth opens more—and I'm certain it will—slip your tongue in a little further. Focus is everything in great sex. Men generally stay focused on one intention. It works! So don't lose yourself in *his* intention and become swept away with *his* focus. Wait . . . Tease . . . Withdraw slowly. If he likes what you're doing and you feel his body rise, carry on with rhythmically bolder strokes, as though you were in the middle of passionate intercourse. When you know for sure that he's following your lead, move on to kiss other areas of his face—his eyes, his nose, his ears. Nibble on his earlobes, his neck, and whatever exposed skin you find.

MASSAGE AND MORE

After all this scrumptious tasting and drawing on his soul, I think now's the time to use his body as a picturesque temple for the high art of massage foreplay. Nothing is more stimulating for your man when done beyond his expectations save fellatio, or hot, heavenly intercourse in his natural position—from behind.

Next, take your time to remove most of your clothing in his full vision. You may want to do a scanty striptease, removing only a few items. Then excuse yourself to don a silky robe with only your sublime nakedness underneath. You will need all of your bodily accoutrements free from any restriction to produce your magnum opus. Beforehand warm the room and the massage oil. It's more thoughtful. And you don't want him to catch a cold as you open much more than his pores.

Exploring your lover's physical being—skin, hair, muscles, lips, and penis—is essential for his pleasure. When done properly it is an undeniable aphrodisiac—

an incredible prelude to lovemaking. It can break the touching barrier while relaxing the body and mind. In minutes, you can soothe, energize, or arouse. You can warm his muscles, loosen tissue, dissolve knots, cramps, and tension. It is the quickest and easiest way to inspire him to open his soul. But he must have trust in you as well as your touch. And the more comfortable you can make him feel, the more he will trust you. When he starts to trust you, his real self will surface. *Trust* is key, especially in successful body massage.

The *first touch* of your fingertips on his skin is the *most important* of all. So take your time—feel him—savor the magic moment when your bodies first connect in massage foreplay. Moreover, this union of skin draws out a man's masculinity and a woman's femininity. If you can imagine that just two and a half square yards of his skin contain five million nerve endings that send sensory signals to his brain with unfathomable speed, you'll better understand why the right touch can feel exquisite.

When you relax a man's brain, he is more apt to open up to you. If you've never done so, it's a good idea to take a look at a skeletal chart. It will help if you visually sketch his outline in your mind before you begin. You will have a better idea of what you're touching. And that helps, believe me.

His skeleton provides the internal framework that supports the rest of his body. He has about 206 bones. His skull encloses and protects his think tank and other important organs, in particular the eyes and inner ears. Gauge the amount of pressure you apply by paying attention to his body language, sighs, moans, and groans. Stay focused and let your sensorial fingers articulate your thoughts—good, positive, generous thoughts that serve to connect your souls.

Give special TLC to the major erogenous zones: the

lips, nipples, and genitals. Tantalize with the musical feel of your fingertips and your tongue. This is only a prelude to the pleasures awaiting him.

Begin your work of art in a heated room with warm oil, unscented or slightly aromatic. Most men are averse to strong smells and greasy liniments. I massage with an oil or lotion of natural ingredients that I include in my romantic kit. I find the subtle, organic scents more palatable to the male taste. Now place a bedsheet or towel over a mat or anything moderately soft. The bed is usually too soft and bare floors are too hard. Your man must feel coddled . . . loved. Relaxing music should be playing in the background, preferably non-vocal. Words might distract.

Ask him to lie down on his stomach. (Most professionals begin with the person on his stomach and I think it works well that way.) Also ask him if he has any injuries before you begin. For example, if he has tendonitis and you unknowingly press and pull, that can hurt him and he will not relax enough to surrender. A lack of surrender will stifle your creativity.

During massage, think of yourself as a sculptor and his body as your clay. Your hands and imagination will mold his clay into a beautiful and fitting tribute to your genius. Use all of his subtle tones and textures to create a golden bronze that would give Michelangelo pause.

Begin: straddle his body so you can have the proper balance and support. Empty some oil into the palm of your left hand and put the bottle down beside you, always within reach. Having access to your lubricant is part of maintaining the massage rhythm. Place both hands on the back of his neck and shoulders, since this is the prominent area where tension is held. Start a rotating motion with your thumbs and fingertips. Gently knead the muscles around, across, and up the neck, into the back of the head, where nerve endings connect, and all around the skull. Spend a lot of time on his head (don't you enjoy a good massage and wash at the beauty shop?), massaging firmly with your fingertips. Then use your nails to gently scratch the scalp. It also feels good to him when you take semilarge sections of his hair and gently tug. As you tug, think of it as pulling out his tension, slowly. Do make sure you tug all the hairs in sections on his entire scalp. It's both healthy and invigorating.

Okay, let's continue back up his spine, rhythmically pumping the muscle with firmer pressure. A good rule is never to let your fingers lose contact with any part of his skin. When a part of you is always touching a part of him, he feels more secure and loved. With the same rhythm, return to the top of the spine and slide both thumbs down the sides of his spinal column. You can feel if he's enjoying your talents. Reverse the movement. Then with the heel of your hands, use a zigzag movement down his spine while blowing air on and kissing each vertebra.

For arms, wrists, and hands, use a squeeze-and-release motion. Squeeze and release—rather firmly—in a pumping kind of motion all the way up to his shoulders, then back down again. Now, spend a lot of time on his hands, those complex organs made up of many small bones. (They're the things he uses the most, other than the obvious thing!) Clasp the sides of one of his hands with both of yours. Use a rotating motion with your thumbs to work in between the palm bones (metacarpals) and finger bones (phalanges). Just feel all portions of his hands.

After you have worked over his torso, gently part his legs and wander on down to the lower half. (No, not that . . . yet!) His buttock muscles will need a much stronger pressure. If your thumbs are tired, alternate with the palms of your hands. Add droplets of oil generously onto his glorious mounds. Push both cheeks together in a rotating rhythm. Lift them and squeeze them. Shape his buttocks with your hands and fingers —lift, separate, and smooth them. Watching and feeling them as you mold your clay is certainly a turn-on, if you know what I mean.

With his legs still parted, rub more oil into his inner thighs. Feel the heat. The craving between his legs will be tormenting, but I'm sure he will let your engaging fingers commence to work the rest of his flesh. His hamstrings in the back of his thighs are likely to be taut; therefore, they need a deeper pressure. As you continue, extend your downward stroke to include the calf muscles and carry on with his Achilles tendons and feet.

You are clearing away all of his thoughts with your seamless changes and variations. That was your intention! Take his foot in your hands and hold it for a few seconds while the nerve endings feel the warmth and energy emanating from your hands. Feel the structure and massage the five long bones of the foot (metatarsals) and toes (phalanges). When you concentrate on his toes, make sure you give each one a gentle tug. From the toes, follow with the instep, ankle, knee, thigh, and up his body once again, but this time using a squeeze-release motion. When you have finished, ask him to turn over on his back or, better still, silently guide him with your hands.

If you happen to get this far, you can continue the massage up and down the front of his entire body, finishing with his head positioned in your lap, gently smoothing the oil into his throat, chest, and shoulders. Then the muscles of his face, temples, brow, eyes, nostrils, and once again . . . his head—which, after all, is a lovely crown for the finale of body massage. He will feel so good lying there in your hands—a passionflower in bloom, readied for your pleasure.

You can enjoy a laid-back, sexy kind of energy in his response. However, in the event your energy is waning, allow for revitalization with tender caresses and sips of chilled champagne. But always have a part of your body touching his. After you feel invigorated, pretend he's the last chocolate éclair you will ever eat. Savoring every nuance, begin to smell, taste, lick, and suck out the creme as if it would be the last time or the first, if you will. While caressing and kissing his neck, shoulders, lips, and face, murmur honest compliments that you sincerely feel from your heart like, "I love the way you taste!" or "I like the feel of your skin!" or "I could drown myself in your manliness."

When you speak with sincerity, he will bathe in the essence. And when you focus on his pleasure, you become liberated. Remember, the only dialogue at this time is flattering and sexy talk, nothing else.

Everything in life is rhythm and timing, as I'm sure you know. Keep in mind the timing of your action and rhythm of the moment. Now for the tongue bath: with silent words of "I love you, I adore you, I worship you" rolling off the tip of your tongue and your soft lips, slowly trace the whole of his anatomy with no stone unturned, and no crevice unattended. To add to his ever growing sensations, you can blow warm air on each spot you lick. Enjoy his delectable manly flavors and smells.

Starting with his fingers, kiss his fingertips, fingers, and the palm of his hand, and hold his hand to your face. Gently put each finger individually into your mouth. Suck and swirl your tongue up and down and around, concentrating on the middle ones as you look deep into his eyes. Let your tongue proceed up his forearm, upper arm, and neck to his hungry mouth. Kiss and gently bite his earlobe while whispering endearing thoughts into his ear like, "Do you like what I'm doing?

Is it okay if I touch you in other places?" Say whatever pure thought your heart is feeling at that moment.

With the tip of your tongue, gently trace the outline of his ear, slightly inserting your tongue at intervals. Don't drown his hearing with a lot of tongue and saliva. That's a sure way to ruin the mood you've been creating.

Whisper sensual and flattering secrets that you've discovered about him while you insert your pointed tongue in the rhythm that you would like your vagina to be penetrated by his penis.

Hmmmmm . . . you certainly know what he's thinking now, right? He has to wait, though, until you are ready. It's not time . . . just yet. Be patient.

You've had a few appetizers, some mouthwatering champagne—now you want to tickle his fancy with yet another delicacy. As you're holding his head in your secure hands, trace your tongue down his neck, planting little kisses as you go. Again, run your fingers through his hair and inhale its aroma. It lets him know that you appreciate all of him as you move down his neck to his pectorals and then his nipples.

A lot of men really enjoy having their pecs massaged (as you did his buttocks—lifting and squeezing), and their nipples sucked, licked, and played with. Others are ultrasensitive and find it rather tickling. If you have a ticklish man, move on. If your man enjoys this procedure (goose bumps on his body are a giveaway), and you'll be able to judge by his reaction as your tongue is sliding in the general vicinity of "the territory"—continue to make love to that area the same way you would like his moist mouth to kiss, suck, and flutter on your sexy breasts and nipples. If he likes it, ever so gently tease the tips of his nipples with the tips of your teeth. Don't bite; rather, gently feel.

For heightened stimulation, you can grasp one of

his nipples between your thumb and index finger, gently rolling it around as you would a grape, without breaking its skin, as your mouth and tongue travel to other areas. Don't forget to alternate from one nipple to the other with the same fervor. Give every part equal attention. You know how you hate it when your guy just sucks one breast all night, while the other is entirely neglected. Don't make the same mistake with him. See, you're showing him in subtle ways how you want it.

At this point, you'll sense how important the right music fits into the layout of your lovemaking. Your body parts dance to the sounds of seduction on his male figure. It only adds to the atmosphere. Without losing tempo, continue with the impression of your soft, moist lips down the sides of his pectorals, rib cage, and belly. Then work your mouth and tongue around his navel area as your hands stroke his thighs, skipping over his genitalia. Remember to tease! At this point, I'd bet my car that your Michelangelo is on the ceiling. Enjoying his response and watching his body come alive in your hands is a definite, if not definitive, reward.

Let your hair and breasts fall and glide around his abdomen, thighs, and accidentally over his groin while your hands stroke and delicately massage his inner thighs. Without touching his penis, kiss all around the area. You're engaging in teasing foreplay before penis play.

Make him hold back while you drive him crazy. He loves it and he hates it. Some men have enormous control. It's challenging to see just how cool they can stay. But others are a bit more expressive. And without warning, the creme in his éclair might suddenly slip out in the middle of your extravaganza. That's actually a compliment to your artistic skill. Nevertheless, it's more exciting when he can last until the last act. But, as the Boy Scouts advise, be prepared!

You've guessed by now what comes next and he's certainly ready, waiting, and deserving. He is absolutely prepared! You have gardened his landscape, made his soul blossom. The time has come to ply your skills in that very special brand of foreplay called fellatio.

FELLATIO

Is that a gun in your pocket or are you just happy to see me?

—MAE WEST

Is fellatio important to men? I can only tell you that almost all the men to whom I spoke told me that fellatio has a place of honor on their wish list. It ties with making love to two women simultaneously as their favorite fantasy. Make it your business to do fellatio so well that he'll forget his ménage à trois. When you really love your man, it's easy to be great!

The other day, as I walked out of a popular chicken diner on Sunset Strip in L.A., I witnessed a pretty "lady of the night" (in this case day) approach two young nice-looking gents in a new white truck. They talked for a few minutes, laughed—when, suddenly, the girl slipped inside the front seat between the boys. The truck pulled to the back of the restaurant in broad daylight, and the girl's head started bopping up and down in a beat, with Snoop Doggy Dogg loudly playing, on both penises. It was amazing. I must confess, I stood there as though I were riveted to the spot . . . watching! Men are visual? Please . . . give me a break!

Some women think "goin' down south" is difficult to do. Actually, you do more difficult things every day. Compared to parallel parking, it's downright easy.

However, you need to know the basics of how his anatomy works. Then, with a little concentration, a lot of practice and self-confidence—*voilà*—good things! Think of it as your favorite food, candy, or ice cream to lick, savor, and play with its flavor. That's a positive step down the bulbous, bronzed path.

For extra fun and play—prime his penis. Do what the geisha do. Get a towel, soap, and warm water, and tenderly wash his sapphire and diamonds. But do it seductively and with great sensitivity. Wash slowly and thoroughly, and talk to it as you tend it.

Now, you're going to play a symphony on his swollen manhood with the orchestra of fellatio. Imagine that you're the great Leopold Stokowski conducting a Stravinsky opus. Your instruments will be his sexual organs in the sensitive rhythms of a violin for handling, a flute for kissing, a clarinet for licking, and timpani for sucking—all orchestrating and conducting a symphony of fellatio.

Usually a symphony is composed in four movements, while the orchestra is divided into different sections (strings, woodwinds, brass, and percussion) to present the creative work.

Fellatio, in a sense, is similar to the colors and harmonies of an orchestrated piece. It usually starts slowly and quietly and builds to a crescendo—an increase in volume. Through the piece, there are highs, lows, ups, and downs—different mood changes, speeds, and rhythms. One minute it flirts, teases, and plays. The next it's passionate, insatiable, and daring. Then it's sensitive, tender, and loving. Feel him. Feel what he wants and give him what he needs.

No matter how sensational a certain action feels, nobody enjoys the same motion on the same spot indefinitely. Variation is the key—spontaneous and rhythmic variation. Whatever music you hear in your mind (whether it be jazz, R and B, soul, rock, Latin, country, or the latest craze), compose with it. Play with your own sense of rhythm and his. Take your time, let things develop instinctively, do not force anything, and be confident. Your sterling skills will tantalize his life force in any rhythmic variation.

HANDLING

Have you ever had a sibling or neighbor take a violin lesson? I have, and believe me, the squawks, squeals, and groans of such a fine instrument in unskilled hands were not only excruciating to my ears, but what about the poor instrument? When a student sticks to the lessons and practices faithfully, what a difference!

A violin, viola, or cello skillfully handled produces mesmerizing music, but only as a result of the right touch. Each musical note is located on a particular string at a specific location. Touching the wrong string will draw the wrong note. Touching the correct string but miscalculating by even a few centimeters spawns a note that is erroneous, sharp or flat, and painful to the ear. And if you happen to touch the right spot on the correct string, too little or too much pressure can cause a dreadful noise. These details are to let you know that when handling your man's instrument the same principles apply.

Handle your lover's penis with the reverence, love, and skill Heifetz bestowed on his violin, Casals his cello, and Segovia his guitar. Their touch came from arduous practice, love of their art, a finely tuned ear, a knowing touch, and the ability to express passion from their heart and soul. The playwright Clifford Odets said, "If you want to be a true artist, you have to see and feel what other people don't." Wise words.

So how *do* you handle a penis? You handle it as if you were holding a Stradivarius. Who will teach you how to play it? Your best "violin teacher" is your man. Ask him to stroke it while you watch. (He may be too shy. If so, let him know that to give him maximum pleasure you need to watch a pro . . . him.)

After watching him stroke, caress, squeeze, admire, and massage his penis, you will be able to mimic the exact grip, area, pressure, and rhythm that he enjoys the most. Pay close attention to every detail, ask questions; educate yourself while mastering his desires.

First, begin by playing scales, slowly graduating to simple melodies, then confidently moving into arpeggios. Only when your lips, mouth, tongue, hands, and fingers make harmonies on his violin will you become the quintessential seductress.

KISSING

Woodwinds are mouthpiece instruments that are more delicate-sounding in character. They can be ethereal and also have a sense of humor.

Create your own sweet sound on his oboe or magic flute with soft, tender kisses from your lips while breathing warm wind across his reed. This is sure to leave him lingering in exotic mystery.

Your lips have tons of nerve endings in them. Use them as sensors. Be a connoisseur who savors that first moment of magnetic contact when your lips first touch his soft flesh. Bathe in the wondrous feeling of intimacy. Taste his juicy desire flowing from the rain-spouting slit in his heavenly helmet. Roll your tongue around the opening as you would roll fine wine on and around your palate.

Since kissing his genitalia is the bosom of familiarity, you want to start slowly by flirting with your lips. Take his breath away and entice him to hold you high in his esteem before you explore the rest of his poetic justice. Allow him to luxuriate in your teasing adventure. Invite him to play, tempt him with artful endeavors.

When your lips meet his crown and glory, kiss it as though you were kissing his parted, hungry lips. Without a doubt, the head and shaft of his penis are the softest part of his body—fine and delicate. It's his treasure chest—the place he stores his gold and lust. When you first cup it in your hands, kiss it lovingly. Appreciate its essence. You may want to close your eyes and yield to his sensuality spreading throughout your body.

Or you may prefer to leave your eyes open and watch his elusive shade formations. Watching is extremely sexy, don't we know? This would be an opportune time to compliment the shape, texture, smell, and feel of his Trojan sword. Admire its intricate design and elegant ridges.

LICKING

The sound of brass instruments will stir the fire in your soul. Their intense, hypnotic notes are notorious for captivating the mind and heart, leaving you spellbound. Why not leave him spellbound the moment you place your mouth and mobile tongue on his trumpet and begin to play? You will feel and see his instrument soar. What glory! What strength! What obedience!

Before you position your mouth to blow, look closely at his member. Imagine a mushroom. After all, a man's penis resembles a mushroom's shape and delicacy. The top of the mushroom is akin to the hood of his penis, the stem of the mushroom is akin to his soft, velvety shaft. The whole of his ne plus ultra, down to his testicles, is extremely sensitive.

Like you, a man must have lubrication. Your wet mouth will always be his first choice. Most men produce their own lubricant, but during fellatio you need an abundance of juicy substance to slide, glide, and tantalize. You want to encourage a flood of artistic expression!

Now imagine that his penis is your favorite aphrodisiac: chocolate truffles, chocolate mousse, tiramisu, butter mints, dark chocolate mints, fruit sorbet, French vanilla ice cream with red, ripe strawberries, loaded with fresh whipped cream, Godiva chocolates, parfaits. Aside from drawing sufficient lubrication from his well, licking his love joy will make him stand firmly at attention, if he's not already.

With the tip of your tongue, circle the mushroom top (called the glans), and then up and down the shaft. The glans is filled with spongy tissue that feels like a woman's inner thigh. The urinary opening (urethral meatus) is the little slit at the top of the head. And the place where the head meets the shaft is called the coronal ridge. (It encircles the base of the glans and is the area where circumcision is performed, if it has been performed.)

The most sensitive part of the whole penile area and the most erotic is the skin within the inverted V, called the frenulum. It's located at the intersection where the head and shaft connect, and it faces away from his body. That's his penile G-spot. (Others are his prostate and perineal areas, but we're concerned with the penis at present.)

Another important area to concentrate on is the tube that runs through the entire length of his penis from the inverted V. It resembles the shaft of an arrow and is known as the urethra; it carries either urine or semen, but don't worry, you won't get a golden shower on top of whipped cream. (Fortunately for you, he's unable to do both simultaneously!) A lot of men are thrilled with a gentle long stroke of your tongue starting at the base of his tube and rolling up to the inverted V, but then an assortment of favorable flutters to focus more on his G-spot.

For variation, play a tune with your tongue by licking around his testicles, then roll your tongue up and down his protrusion while intermittently changing your pattern to a rapid fluttering all around his crown. Alternate with kisses and exploring licks. But remember to keep most of your focus on his G-spot. That will always produce a melody he won't forget.

SUCKING

The percussion section of the orchestra provides the beat—the pulse. A throbbing begins at your female center and spreads throughout your entire womanhood. You'll feel the birth of your body's rhythm from Miami to Zimbabwe. You'll long to move to a certain beat— to dance, to express.

Have you ever passed a concert hall or church where the music has measure and your head starts bopping, or your foot begins to tap to the beat? Just yesterday while I was driving in my car, a big black Bronco pulled up beside me at a red light. The music blaring from the driver's stereo was so infectious that, without realizing, I found my fingers strumming his beat on my steering wheel. The driver obviously sensed that I was enjoying his bass, because when I looked up, he was smiling. Finding your man's rhythm is easy. Just listen to his preferred music and latch onto the beat. Then give him what he likes.

A reminder: in a great piece of music or work of art, start slowly and build. Feel the emotion, ride his wave of desire. You're not going for speed. You're going for gold. Don't go all the way down on his shaft too soon. Don't use harsh, rapid stroking, with vacuum cleaner suction. Don't use quick, jerky movements, sharp teeth, or fingernails . . . *please*. It's not a ham sandwich! And also remember that he needs a wealth of lubrication, especially as you increase the tempo, adapting to the intensity of his fervor.

We know his right brain is visual. Let him look, feel, and hear the seduction. Give him the pleasure of watching his timbales being played. Let him revel in the hedonistic joy of your gifts. When Mr. Vesuvius decides to erupt, it will be a generous flow of warm, orgasmic lava.

After you have kissed and licked his penis sufficiently, hold the base of it with one hand while your other hand gently strokes the swollen member (recall the handling section above), and place your mouth on the head and delicately suck. Continue to tease him by going very slowly, gracefully sliding your mouth up and down, up and down. He needs to anticipate your charms. Use your most valued agents—teasing, flirtation, and mystery. Together with true love, these components are the basis of seductive lovemaking—an intrinsic and vital part of your symphony.

At this point in your sucking, you can begin to use your throat as a receptacle for the tip of his penis. Whether the complete penis can be taken into the whole of the throat depends entirely on your gag reflex, whether it's hyperactive, mild, or absent. Most women I interviewed said that when they relaxed, became uninhibited and totally involved, they were able to take the penis into the deepest parts of their throat.

Vary your techniques during the course of fellatio. Suck and lick a while; then suck and simultaneously stroke the shaft with one hand, while your opposite hand caresses his testicles. The point is be inventive, mix it up, and most of all *have fun*!

If you're having fun, it's almost a given that your man is going to be having fun, too. Several men that I interviewed talked about what it was like to be on the receiving end. Harry, for example, a forty-six-year old successful screenwriter, gives his view of why he likes "deep throat" and what he feels are the electrical connections: "It's like acupressure. You touch a spot, it has a response; you touch two spots, it has another response; you touch three spots, it gives you a totally different response. When my penis goes all the way down into my woman's throat, I feel a suction and an envelopment around the head. I also feel a suction and pressure at the base of my penis where it joins at the balls. That's why it's such a total turn-on, both of these things are happening simultaneously. Talk about all-encompassing. Man!!!"

It's possible to create a facsimile by taking your hand and making a ring out of the first finger and thumb. Place that at the base of the cock and, for support, apply gentle but firm pressure while working on the head of the penis with your mouth.

"Deep throat" is not such a no-no anymore. In this day and age it's often par for the course. No matter what size a man's penis (of course within reason), it can be done, but it must be learned. Compare it to swallowing a big chunk of food. You really don't think about it, do you? Well, it's the same with a man; he's just flesh. Begin by loosening the muscles of your throat.

Learning "how to" and practicing is the key, just as your fella has to learn to be your "little raspberry" by practicing the coordination of his tongue muscles. He wants to be the best at satisfying you during cunnilingus. So when he sent you to nirvana with his expertise and technique, you didn't think his van Goghlike strokes of the tongue were from a novice. Oral lovemaking is definitely not something that comes naturally to every guy or gal. So practice, practice, practice.

RHYTHM

After you become familiar with the various aspects of pleasing his penis, you need to find the right rhythm for him. Rhythm is like a heartbeat or the underlying pace in music. It's smooth, flowing, sensual, and romantic—we're not talking 78 rpm on the turntable here!

With rhythm in mind, cup his testicles with one hand, hold his shaft with the other hand, and put your mouth around his head. Now one hand gently massages his testicles while your head and other hand are going up and down in the same direction with the same tempo.

For rhythmic variation, you can move your hand up and down on his shaft, independently of your mouth, which is licking and sucking his head, while your other hand gently massages his testicles and central perineum (another erogenous area between the scrotum and anus). This latter requires more skill and, at first, sounds uncoordinated, but is really analogous to a poly-rhythmic African dance that synthesizes several seemingly different body movements into a unified whole. It can only be done if you and your lover are really in tune with each other—emotionally, mentally, physically, and spiritually. At such a point the common rhythm in your souls coalesce. This rarity is reserved for the fortunate and is the kind of sexual chemistry that transcends eroticism.

You've probably never milked a cow or even had the pleasure of seeing one being milked. But if you haven't, make an effort to do so. It's invigorating. You sit on a little stool in front of the cow's udder and put both of your hands on her teats. (Using a special ointment helps.) Start from the top of the teat and, in a controlled manner, actively work all five of your fingers, drawing the milk out in a form of massage. Pull in a rhythmic sequence—left, right, left, right. Latching on to a perfect rhythm is an unforgettable experience for you and the cow.

Animals understand a natural rhythm—men understand a natural rhythm. It's really that simple. An animal will not object to a confident pull, nor will your man object if you are confident. He gets nervous when you appear self-conscious and insensitive while doing the act, or pull too harshly with one hand, or fumble with your fingernails or teeth on his sensitive skin. If you did that to a cow, she would kick you in the mouth with her hoof; fortunately, a man is more kind. He just squirms, grits his teeth, and holds his breath, hoping you'll stop hurting him and find a more conducive stride.

Pace yourself and don't forget to breathe. Begin with soothing, gentle strokes, then as he responds, you can be a little more firm and aggressive. If you feel his penis becoming engorged and you taste or feel fluid flowing from the opening in the tip, it could be a sign that he's close to ejaculation . . . sometimes. You need to look at the expression on his face from time to time and pay close attention to his moans and groans. He will definitely let you know how fast, how slow, how pleasurable the experience. His body and verbal language are your guiding lights to the end of his tunnel.

In addition, you may want to observe how he's caressing your head, hair, face, mouth. Unconsciously, most men start to move in their own rhythm. Sometimes, they will gently move your head in the rhythm they desire. So if he's pleased with your composition, continue. If you see, feel, or hear that he may be in pain, *stop instantly*! You may be hurting him. And if this is one of your early lovemaking experiences, your man may be too shy, embarrassed, or macho to let you know that he's in pain. Don't be afraid to ask if everything is okay. It will not alienate your man, but, in fact, make you all the more resplendent to him.

SEMEN

A man's semen has the faint taste and texture of clam sauce in a bowl of pasta. Very, very few men have the taste of a persimmon, which is to say sweet. You're a lucky lady if your man has the "drink of the gods," which is similar to the nectar of a honeysuckle.

There are many factors involved; but most probably, the taste of semen is determined by diet or stress. A large intake of amino acids, a lot of salt, herbs, vitamins, garlic, curry, et cetera, can cause strangeness in its flavor; sometimes a large intake of pineapple juice can produce a sweetness. If your fella has a sour or bitter taste all the time and it displeases your senses, don't try to swallow—you'll probably gag. Off the record, when a man's semen has a sour taste, it can mean he's had an orgasm recently, possibly through masturbatory means. If he ejaculates more than twice in one session for a day or two, he may also become a little sour or acidic.

Different men ejaculate different textures of semen. To draw an analogy, the yolk of an egg has more viscosity than the egg white. Right? How about the analogy of icing on a cake? Some cakes have thick frosting, others a thin glaze that dribbles down the side. Your man's semen may be as viscous as thick egg yolk or frosting, whereas other men's semen may be similar to the thinner egg white or glaze. The point is that consistency does not dictate flavor.

SWALLOWING

Swallowing is not an obligatory thing. Don't ever think you have to swallow if you don't want to—end of sentence! Also, don't ingest on a full stomach. You'll be sorry.

If your guy is having a hard time ejaculating and you're starting to get lockjaw because you've lost that "lovin' feeling" . . . stop! Unless, of course, you've become Spartan just to prove the point of orgasm, which is not terribly exciting, but rather mechanistic.

In the event he absolutely cannot ejaculate, don't worry about it. He's only human. Just maybe, he had a hard day at work; he's worried; he had one too many beers. Maybe he masturbated earlier while thinking about your overwhelming beauty. Or maybe he was ready to come and you unknowingly changed rhythms. That'll do it every time! However, once a man starts to ejaculate, his apparatus functions in such a way that he cannot stop, even if he wants to. It's a runaway train!

Swallowing the fluids of the man you love is akin to fulfilling yourself in a matrimonial exchange of soul. It's the closest thing to penile insertion that a woman can do. Whereas a man can insert his penis into his woman's vagina, a woman has nothing to insert into her man; swallowing can substitute. The easiest way to swallow is to keep the head of his penis at the back of your throat and, as he pulsates and spurts out semen, gulp it down using the back of your throat in a rapid rhythm. As he squirts, you swallow quickly. And don't think about anything else but opening the throat to receive.

This unabashed enthusiasm is definitely not shared by all women. Unless great love or lust supersedes, women in general will not suck or swallow a man's semen. Therefore, ingestion is the ultimate sign of acceptance (unless, of course, he's paying for it).

Aside from swallowing semen, women often rub it on their faces and breasts for a few reasons: love; nastiness; pure adult lust; or desire for a natural facial, similar to an egg-white protein mask used for cleansing and rejuvenation. At any rate, handling semen is a sensitive issue all around. The male psyche is more fragile than you might suspect. When he offers a gift of his precious fluids, any form of rejection is a slap to the face of his manhood. Lovers must be sensitive to these particular needs.

If you should decide to swallow, you will be bestowing on your lover the ultimate sign of acceptance. Given that you want to give him this gift, is it safe? In this day and age, I'm obliged to warn you that swallowing is safe if your partner is healthy. According to the most current data available, it's not the semen that transmits disease; it's blood from an open sore or a cut. However, data change every day. Let me remind you that the act of love about which I am writing and which I am supporting applies only to monogamous, trusting relationships.

FELLATIO FOR THE NOVICE

You've probably been programmed to think: "Don't put that thing in your mouth. It's nasty and dirty." Change your programming to: "What a delicious new food! Why, it tastes like a bonbon. I want more! More!! More!!!"

Above all, don't be afraid. His penis will not harm you. Quite the contrary, it will love you if you treat it well. Like his finger, toe, or nose, it's part of his anatomy. Needless to say, the most important part! The most supple part!

The way a penis operates is truly fascinating. It can swell in a matter of seconds—go from very little to very big with just your gaze. In Trinidad they say, "The penis is the lightest thing in the world. Even a thought can make it rise." Don't you think that his "expression of desire" is a wonder of the world? It's so delicate in feel, yet when it's firm and throbbing, it can be tough and hard. Because he loves it, you should grow to love it, too.

I can never talk too much about cleanliness. It should be a given. If not, do as the experienced lovers. Always work showering or bathing separately or together into your dates. Oftentimes, washing one another is a sensual part of lovemaking. For example, if you bring your date home, tell him to relax, then seductively whisper in his ear that you're going to slip into something more comfortable. You know you're going to clean yourself, right? The same idea for your man. When he brings you to his home, he usually offers you a drink while he excuses himself to either wash off or take a quick shower. Providing you know for a fact that you're both clean, you might use the time to undress and slide into bed.

Suffice it to say, you may encounter some residue of urine, sweat secretions, body odors, and so forth. In which case, do as I suggested earlier: fetch a warm, soft rag, warm water, and delicate soap. Seductively wash his entire genitalia. It is a part of foreplay, especially among the famous courtesans. When done expertly, it's deliciously arousing. The gentle washing gives you a chance to introduce your charming self to his miracle of life, and also to investigate the miracle. Lather his lovables with slippery suds and wash with tender strokes. Talk to it, if you feel the incentive. Only when you're ready, tenderly stroke your cheek, nose, and eyes with his tip and shaft. Maybe this caressing contact will dispel any bogus myths about his organ.

Take a few drops of unscented cream and gently massage along the shaft of his penis and sac containing his testicles. Feel what you're touching. Explore with all your senses. It will be a pleasurable experience for him and for you, too.

A few rules to remember: Develop mutual trust and comfort by starting slowly and gradually building. Please don't go from zero to sixty in five seconds with an up-and-down, up-and-down stroke as if it were a race to the finish. Pace the action. The slower you go, the bigger his "trumpet lily" will grow. Be loving. Be patient. It takes time and the right rhythm for a man to have an orgasm. No woman wants a man to go straight for her clitoris and turn on the vacuum. No man wants a woman to dive straight for his whole piano and hammer on his keyboards with frantic strokes. Actually, they hate that. Relax. They want to bathe in the poetic feelings—from the stroking with your hands, lips, and mouth to the rubbing and admiring. All mouth doesn't work. You can't blow his live instrument without using your breath, tongue, lips, fingers, hands, and whole being to siphon beautiful music. Allow him to grow in your hands and mouth while you explore the delicate, tender, smooth flesh of his manhood.

Lubrication is absolutely necessary to avoid chafing his sensitive area with multi-stroking. Best is your own saliva, but for fun you can use honey, jam, jelly, whipped cream, maple syrup, caramel, chocolate syrup, and all flavors of ice-cream toppings for his cone. Pick your flavor.

Sucking requires actual entry of the penis into the deeper parts of your mouth. Just as the penis enters your vagina little by little, so the penis should enter your mouth gradually while you are loving and adoring it—in and out, in and out, gently. I'll keep reminding you, don't forget to tease. To tease is to please.

As time goes by, the penis can be taken in more deeply, but only as you feel comfortable. If your man's penis is extremely large or if your mouth hurts when he enters, use a different approach. Lubricate his penis with your saliva, then circle his hood and V with your tongue. Start licking and nibbling on his hood and down the length of his member while cupping the top and caressing it gently with the inside of your palm. You need to use your hands in this situation. Cup both hands, caress around the top, and nibble around the sides. Maybe his penis is too wide and too curved. Then you need to put both hands gently around the top while licking down its body. Once you work your way down, don't neglect his testicles. Cup them gently with your hands while your open mouth licks the lower part of the shaft. The reason you must have your hands around him is to bridle in his passion if he happens to start bucking out of control. In a millisecond, he could go from a trot into a full gallop. Be warned that your hands should be in command at all times to corral the situation, otherwise your mouth could feel a stampede.

A normal penis can reach into the deepest part of your throat. Use your hand around the base of his shaft to control the depth of penetration. Most men feel good if you use one hand on their shaft and the other hand to gently caress and feel their testicles.

Now, let's not forget that some men ejaculate somewhat quickly, and there will be times you wish he would. Most men manufacture a substance called pre-ejaculatory fluid first. Acquiring a taste for semen is like cultivating a taste for wine or beer. Some people don't particularly care for wine or beer at first, but after several stages of tasting, they acquire a true liking or even a passion. During the evolution of your palate, take small tastes of semen at first. You can use water, wine, Binaca breath drops, or the chaser of your choice to cleanse your mouth. In time you will build toward a more complete consumption.

During your next lovemaking session, experiment

in the same manner. When he comes, taste some of it, but don't swallow. Keep it in your mouth and then use a towel or sheet or whatever you have near you to let him expel the rest of his semen while you're acquiring a taste. Or if there's nothing to wipe with, let it drop out of your mouth onto your chest, if you prefer. The key is don't be afraid to take it out of your mouth. He will certainly understand.

The third time you're together, be adventurous. Take a gulp and you will see it's just like milk gravy. Not bad, really. It's simply a matter of getting accustomed to doing it. And I believe these tips will direct you on a new, fun, and daring journey.

You may ask yourself, "How does it feel in the mouth just before he comes? How do I create a rhythm when swallowing? Or, how long do I continue?" The signal is when his penis becomes extremely tense and inflexible. There are definite lines of engorgement along its sides, the glans pulsates and becomes top-heavy as it contracts. Throbbing is key. Take some advice from the comedians in Las Vegas: "You keep on lickin' till it stops tickin'!"

However, some men have severe sensitivity and find it difficult to ejaculate with any motion. They will usually grab your head and/or your hand to give pause while their sperm flows freely.

It's best not to let the semen sit in your mouth and then swallow. Rather, when the semen shoots, gulp it down as quickly as you can. You create a rhythm by pulling the head of his penis out of your throat into your mouth cavity and pushing it back against your throat—all the while swallowing rapidly. You can feel when a supply of semen is pushing through the urethra, because the glans will pulsate. Continue to swallow in rhythm.

FELLATIO FOR THE ADVANCED

To complete this section, I offer an advanced technique of fellatio. While you take him on your fantastic voyage, let your hair and breasts fall and brush all around his abdomen, thighs, and over his groin, while your hands stroke and delicately massage his inner thighs. Without touching his penis, kiss all around those same areas. Welcome him to penis foreplay!

Now lightly kiss his glans, shaft, and scrotum while your hands fondle the surrounding area. Position yourself over him so you'll have more control of what you're preparing to do. It's sexy for both of your legs to straddle one of his. That way you can massage your own clitoris with his leg as you go through the various stages of loving.

Ever so gently, take his penis in both of your hands and admiringly caress it against your face. Look lovingly at its shape, color, size, aroma, and texture, all blossoming into full maturity from your nurturing. Compliment and talk to it while sliding it against your lips, cheeks, eyes, and throat. You say the things that you feel and mean. Like, "Hmmmm, you smell so good. You feel so big and firm in my hands. I want to taste you. I want to put you in my mouth and rub my tongue all over your head, especially that tender spot. Then I want to take it down my throat. I want to lick your come like melting candy. I want you to rain all over me. You make me wetter than the Mississippi River. I can't wait for you to explode in my mouth!" This is just an example of what you might verbalize, if it's true and comfortable for you.

Now's the time to do all the things you told him you were going to do. Continue teasing. Play and suck and lick around his nipples, stomach, and legs, passing by his penis. Then start to play with his balls. (Again:

some men don't like their balls played with or squeezed, but most men do.)

Begin nibbling and kissing the tip of his penis along the shaft and over the testicles. Give the entire groin area your complete focus and total attention. While holding his property in one hand and gently massaging it, kiss in between the folds or creases where the groin starts.

Okay, enough teasing. Here's where we really begin. As Candy Sample likes to say, "It's serious cocksucking time!" Lick and kiss the hood and shaft of his penis with your moist lips, making sure everything gets wetter than wet. You can never get it too wet, as I'm sure you know. Even the ooh-ahh sounds of saliva mixed with sucking are hot for him. You are letting your man know that his penis is being worshiped at the altar of a love goddess.

Did I mention that you need to look into his eyes once in a while? You do. It will be your barometer of appreciation. I can't imagine at this point that he would be in pain, but one never knows when the stakes are high. Maybe he's excruciatingly ticklish and everything except sucking tickles him. Don't rule that out. Paying close attention to his body language and checking the expressions on his face regularly help you on your journey. As I said earlier, every man is different, and if your man is ticklish, give him time to learn and trust your loving and sensitive hands. He'll come around eventually. It's all about *trust*.

After your saliva has gotten him wetter than an Amazonian rain forest, sucking will be comfortable and fun. Always start at the top and work your way down, neglecting nothing. Everything should be slow and easy, building to a crescendo. Remember the symphony!

Every move, stroke, lick, and suck must have a melody, a rhythm, a flow all its own. With one hand on his shaft, the other hand on his testicles, and your mouth wrapped around the hood, the rapture expands. Men need reassurance, so continue talking to his animated member with mmmmms, ahhhhs, and ooohhs— inhaling and stroking, kissing and blowing on it. Be honest! If you think it's big, tell him how big and beautiful it is. If not, compliment other things you sincerely like, maybe the shape, color, or smoothness. If you love him, you'll love it. Compliments will make him feel proud. But he needs truthful communication, not just blind sex. Blind sex is like eating bland rice cakes as an aphrodisiac. It doesn't wear well.

With one hand still wrapped around his shaft, the other on his testicles, and your mouth around the hood, slide, slide, slip and slide—up and down, up and down. Your head and hand are moving in the same direction, as your other hand massages his sac to the same rhythm. It's as if your hand and mouth form a tunnel with a soft wet suction at the top, or a sheath filled with a slippery substance in which his penis is inserted and massaged. You start with an hum pa pa, hum pa pa, hum pa pa, hummm. Recall milking the cow. It must be done with confidence and a smooth rhythm. Be confident that you're gentle; that you know what you're touching; that you've discovered his desired pressure; and that you're in sync with his body language. His penis is coming alive and pulsating in your hand.

If he's growing bigger and bigger and a few oohs and ahhs are escaping his lips, or inaudible words are being murmured, then you know you're breathing spring into his happy seasons.

Another great inspiration for this day of reckoning is when you make tiny circles with your lubricated thumb around his inverted V, as your mouth and tongue suck and lick his glans.

After you know that he is slippery wet, circle your

erect nipple around his secretions at the slit in the top of his penis. You can gently hold it open while your nipple peeks further inside. Then do it with the other nipple. Let him look. He loves to look! If you have ample breasts, put his penis in your cleavage; squeeze the breasts together in an up-and-down massage, catching onto his penis's rhythm. Make sure there's plenty of oil or saliva in between your breasts and on his tip and shaft. Keep these playful parts as wet as possible.

Rub his penis on your cheek and circle it around your mouth. Kiss and lick all around his shaft and balls, slightly pulling his testicles into your mouth with a very, very delicate sucking motion. Be extra careful not to hurt this area. Some men prefer it harder, most don't. Sensitively ask and explore to find out what your man likes. He'll tell you, I'm sure.

After you've used all your senses and different pacing, pressures, and strokes with your hands, mouth, and tongue; after you've exhausted your erotic repertoire and are totally satiated; after gratifying yourself and your lover: put one hand at the base of his cock and push down on his sac to show him how long his rock-hard organ is now that it's been thrilled by your aggressive, knowing composition. Keep it pressed down while you take the fingers of your other hand and gently swirl them around his juicy top as you look deep into his eyes with your throaty voice asking, "Darling, where do you want to come? Do you want to come on my breasts, my face, my stomach? Do you want me to drink you? Or do you want a piece of my apple pie?"

If he can even think at this point, I'm sure he will say, *"Anything you want!!!!"*

Now, don't take advantage of his vulnerable condition and ask him for the moon, the stars, and rain every minute. That's not nice or kind. Don't use the intimate gift of surrender to barter or trick. Lovemaking is pure and holy. Plus you'll lose his trust, the asset you took so long to earn.

Angles in all forms of lovemaking are very important. Maybe you want to be positioned at an angle for deeper swallowing. When your lover is ready to come, having his penis all the way at the back of your throat is best for direct shooting. There, his spurting penis will feel like someone is simply shooting water down your throat; the reflex to swallow is all you'll feel. Always keep your hand around the shaft so your firm grip can control the rhythm and penetration of the situation.

He may scream, have body spasms, and let out primitive sounds during his orgasm. It's such a spiritual release for him when you push all his sexual buttons simultaneously. Also, during ejaculation, it's sexy for him if you massage his central perineum, the area between his testicles and anus. A light rubbing or slight massage encourages a more enjoyable orgasm.

I don't want to get into the anus right now because that's such an individual call. But again, some men love the whole idea of your inserting a lubricated finger to slightly massage their prostate just before they begin to achieve orgasm. When done professionally, it will blow him away. However, other men are just too embarrassed to participate in that particular activity. Ask him seductively whether he so desires.

When all is said and entirely done, you may want to delicately kiss the top of his penis and tell him how much you love him. As I'm sure you know, the above experience is best when there is passion between kindred spirits, great love, chemistry, and enthusiasm for one another. Never be uptight and repressed about loving your man. Savor, relish, wallow in your passions without shame. You have just evoked a delicious sensation of arousal—yours and his. Be proud of your talents and communication skills.

Fellatio is a large part of loving your man completely. It's truly an art when done to his desired and erotic expectations. When you become his magnificent seductress, he will forget his ménage à trois fantasy.

Love is a total release of all the senses; and like beauty, it is in the body of the beholder. Two people in love have the right to do anything that pleases both of them. Love is never judgmental. Everything I've discussed only applies to *real love*. That's the only time you can create heavenly music.

Men generally love receiving fellatio, partly because the act itself is pure pleasure and partly because they don't feel the performance pressures they often feel during intercourse. You are his "lady of the night," his dream come true. So do allow your man his pleasure. He deserves it! And in return, he will kiss and lick you from head to toe, devouring every moist and succulent inch of you in an unabashed orgy of lust, love, and gratitude that will leave you in a limp, sweaty, smiling state of bliss.

INTERCOURSE

When you engage in intercourse, you enter into a mystery as deep as the ocean; as old as time; as new as the birth of the present moment; as vast as the universe; and as near as the heart of your lover lying beside you. It's been experienced by human beings since before they even understood that they were human beings. It's an eternal dance in which all things in nature take part, and it's been going on since before the beginning of what we understand to be time.

I marvel at the lyricism of butterflies. Only minutes ago, I looked outside my window and was enchanted to witness the duet of a male and female butterfly mating in the warm wind. It seemed as if the male was riding on the wings of the female. They were so tightly connected that, at first glance, they appeared to be one—floating in the same rhythm as would a rose petal if it were dropped from the Eiffel Tower.

With this thought in mind, let us move on to the composition and choreography of intercourse. Foreplay was the rehearsal—now you dance . . . Feel your bodies vibrate to the sensuous rhythms of your minds—music created by the two of you together that no one else can hear. That's the miracle of your duet. So listen carefully to the music that weaves your dance of lovemaking. It will make the difference between a satisfying orgasm and no orgasm at all!

Each person has an individual style of dance. Some dances are as carefully choreographed as the Ballet Russe, while others are as primal and abandoned as a pagan fertility rite. You want to have both of those styles and everything in between too in your sexual repertoire.

Watch how people move on a dance floor. Some couples are as smooth as silk, others look like wild mustangs, shaking their heads, arms, and feet to God knows what music. Oftentimes, I wonder exactly what sound those individuals are hearing. But give them credit. They do hear something. They've surrendered to "it" and are expressing themselves with a vitality and courage that promise extraordinary delights in the evening ahead.

Since there is an array of personal styles, techniques, and accoutrements in lovemaking, you must follow your own instincts as did Martha Graham and other trailblazers of dance. Your instincts will never let you down. If you and your lover prefer drifting in an easy, relaxing, mesmerizing tide, move to that sensation; if you enjoy jazz, find that tempo; if you fancy blues, rap, rock and roll, or country, find that cadence. Follow the natural rhythms that belong exclusively to you and your lover. No one can teach you that. It's innate. Explore and experiment with one another's whims, desires, and fantasies. You bring your interpretation, he brings his, and then when your sex organs finally meet and merge, your emotional centers unite and spin into a soaring spiral that spills into the night.

Sometimes, Prince Charming will take you in his arms and lead your glass-slippered Cinderella around the ballroom floor while you gaze lovingly into his spellbinding eyes during a Strauss waltz. Did you know that during the Regency period the waltz was considered too risqué for young maidens? Although we smile at the thought, the guardians of virtue of that period were not fools. Just think of it. All that twirling and spinning around, having a lady's breath taken away while being firmly held in the arms of a beautiful man was very exciting. Isn't it still?

A visual pantomime of seduction can be seen by Fred Astaire and Ginger Rogers in the film *Gay Divorcée* as they dance to "Night and Day." He tries to draw her close. She withdraws. He tries again. She becomes interested and allows him nearer. They touch and begin to move. By the end of the dance they're spinning together over the shining surface of the floor —her skirt billowing and floating all around them in celebration.

Watch Torville and Dean dancing on ice to their gold-medal interpretation of *Bolero*. Who could miss the eroticism of that build in intensity and the ending that might be "death" or merely the state of being "spent" that follows climax?

Check out the film *Romeo and Juliet* starring the premier danseur Rudolf Nureyev with Margot Fonteyn. Everything that can be expressed about romantic and erotic love can be seen in their interpretation of that ballet. The power of their genius enables you to see the joining of not only their bodies but also their spirits and souls. They show to the public what you and your lover will do to each other in private.

As a dancer of love, you need to prepare. Do you think Nijinsky could make his breathtaking leaps on legs that weren't superbly conditioned by exercise? Well, your vagina is a muscular organ; hence, the more you exercise it properly, the better conditioned it will be to pleasure both you and your man.

Your pleasure muscle—pubococcygeus or PC—extends from front to back across your pelvic walls. It supports your bladder and surrounds the urinary, vaginal, and anal passages.

Let's get those muscles into condition by exercising them! They're the same ones you use to start and stop urination. Contract—hold—release. Do sets of fifteen to thirty, three to five times a day, any time, any place —in the car, at a board meeting, or in line at the grocery store.

After a few weeks, you will be able to latch onto his penis like a loving boa constrictor. You, in turn, will more easily feel his thickness growing inside. Also during orgasm the involuntary muscular contractions of your uterus will be stronger. That's good! The strength, dexterity, and mobility with which you use your PC muscles can either take him to a Paphian paradise or a horizontal ride around the block. It's your trip.

There are sex shops that have tiny balls or a lightweight bar bell designed for exercising your PCs. However, it might be a lot more fun to let your lover participate in your "exercise program." He inserts his finger slowly into your vagina and you practice gripping and releasing around his finger. He can begin to feel how proficient you become after a few sessions. You want to duplicate this exact motion when he's inside. The idea is to grip his penis with your vaginal muscles as he slides out, then relax as he reenters. Once you catch on to the rhythm, you can't beat it. But most of all, he will think a thousand fingers are massaging him to orgasm.

Now that you've thoroughly prepared your vagina to make love to his penis, there's something that he needs to do to prepare his penis to enter your vagina. That is, of course, if you're not in a monogamous relationship, which I hope you are.

Scenario: You think it's love, because it's definitely hot and heavy. You're ready for the big moment. He didn't bring a condom. *Stop!!* Lovingly and firmly explain that you both may think you're disease-free, but people can be "positive" and not know it. You also need a condom to protect you against pregnancy and other transmittables. Be safe and keep a supply on hand. Or if you prefer, use a female condom until both of you are tested. Simply tell him that the precaution protects you both, since you care so much about one another. Enough.

Now you're both ready to make love. Hold him in your arms, caress him, kiss him, and treat him as the totally special and unique discovery that he is. Before he glimpses heaven's gate, respond to him as if it were the first time. Every way you touch his body or move your pelvis with "him" inside should be a new experience—every time you love him. You can't lose with this attitude!

Ignore all rules that make men active and women passive. After you come together, each partner will usually take a turn at the lead before returning back to a central unified rhythm. You create and choreograph as you go along, mutually inspiring one another with equal parts imagination, flair, energy, reverence, and passion—ending in total fulfillment.

The beauty of intercourse is in the magical flow of positions—the endless gliding of two units in one synchronized rhythm. Think of your vagina as Ginger's arms wrapped around and holding on to Fred's confident and secure penis while he glides you around the floor in different rhythms, tunes, and dance steps. You never miss a beat. You feel nurtured in his gentle yet firm embrace.

At the most basic level, there are really two positions of intercourse: horizontal and vertical—up and down. However, there are many variations on these two themes that you and your lover can discover when your bodies are attuned. Positions should be comfortable and satisfying for both of you at all times.

Most of the women with whom I've spoken say that there are three basic positions in which they can achieve orgasm: missionary, woman on top, or doggy. Men are slightly more adaptable, preferring doggy style or woman on top, followed by any and all positions in which they can achieve ejaculation comfortably. It's individual.

Permit me to offer a few more suggestions in the event you have only experienced one or two positions. And please don't hesitate to guide your lover through a few of the movements listed below. It will be an artistic endeavor. Learning positions is comparable to doing pliés at a ballet barre. After you warm up properly, if he's willing and you're able, you will make toe tap-

pin', power packin', soul possessin', mind messin' love
. . . until you catch your breath for more!

The choreography of the first few positions before
doggy style (where he will need to pull out) offers
choices of movement while staying solidly connected.
When you shift, move slowly and keep the rhythm. This
fluid connection will sweep you both toward the sweet
madness of overwhelming gladness.

THE MISSIONARY POSITION

I feel the most important position to experience orgasm
at the same time is the missionary. With his manly body
atop your feminine self, you can look into each other's
eyes and gradually create a gentle, soft pulse that builds
and builds, until you both explode into the high-voltage
concurrent orgasm—the stuff dreams are made of.

In the missionary, you're lying flat on your back
with your legs apart. Your man is over you with his
knees bent or stretched, appearing to be doing a push-
up between your open legs. Resting his body weight on
his elbows and knees, he can touch your breasts with
his free hands and suck on your nipples as his penis
penetrates your vagina.

The key is flow. Some bodies fit and flow perfectly
together. Other bodies need to experiment with positions several times before shouting hallelujah! But while
dancing to the music, take care not to overextend your
anatomy with too much enthusiasm. It could cause
injury.

So, you're on your back, right? There's little variation on this theme except for his flexibility and the
mobility of your legs and, of course, the possibility of
jackknifing your spine. For example, your knees can be
bent with your feet on the bed; your legs can be
wrapped around his waist, pulling up your lower torso
for better control; in the same wraparound leg position,

let the heels of your feet encircle his buttocks, pressing him into you rhythmically; tuck your toes under his calves for firmer support.

Your hands can gently guide his torso back, preparing him for your legs to go over his shoulders. One leg can be over his shoulder while the other hangs loose; your straight legs can be opened outward almost into a side split; your knees can be pulled in close to your chest or to the sides of your upper torso.

THE SCISSORS POSITION

This adaptation actually looks like two pairs of open scissors meeting at the center. Without him pulling out, gently coax his torso back over your body in the stretched-out missionary once again. This readies him for another modification—the scissors.

Straighten out your left leg as your left hand gently guides his right knee over that leg and in between your armpit close to your left breast. After he's positioned, pull your knees up. This will encourage his buttocks to rise giving him more support as he shifts onto his knees. Now . . . he can more easily pump your pelvis to the rhythm he desires. You too can enjoy the shakin' and bakin' of a sexy ride.

When you've exhausted the scissors position, return to the flat missionary by stretching out your left leg and sliding it underneath his right leg. Circle your legs around his waist and with both hands gently push his chest back so that his buttocks are sitting on his heels.

LEGS OVER SHOULDER

Lift your legs high in the air over his shoulders and point your toes. Your free fingers can circle around the base of his penis in lubricated massage while alternately stimulating his balls.

SITTING POSITION

With his knees bent and him seated back on his heels,
clasp your hands around the back of his neck and slide
onto his lap. Your legs can either fall over his legs freely
or circle his torso with your feet clasped together. This
will give you tremendous security for the ride.

While you're still facing each other, he can lift you
up with his body weight, simultaneously straightening
his upper torso. With his strong hands hoisting your
buttocks higher and closer into his penis, his mouth can
suck on your breasts and nipples as he continues to
pump in his rhythmic flow. This position is still his ball
game. You're a loving participant enjoying his lead.

You may want to reverse the love flow. Same position, but you hang onto his torso while he straightens
out his legs. Go very slowly and be careful he doesn't
slip out. He can lean back onto his arms, supporting
himself as you bring your torso down with your weight
on your knees. Then you can ride him, encircling his
neck with your right arm and holding onto his right
knee with your left arm concurrently. It puts you in the
driver's seat.

WOMAN ON TOP

Sitting on top of him, reach your arms back, holding
onto his ankles for support as he massages your breasts.
Now release his legs. Then smoothly straighten the entire length of your body over his. Your body weight can
be completely on top of his. In this position you can
feel the thickness and length of his penis sliding in and
out. This is an excellent time to squeeze and release
your buttock muscles as he slips in and out. You can
also control the exact amount of his penis you want to
take inside. Your elbows can support your body weight
as you lean forward and kiss his lips and slide your

pubic bone over his for maximum sensation. Often-times, this motion massages your clitoris and stimulates you to a quickened orgasm or two.

This would be a good time to lift yourself up while he is completely stretched out. Squat over him with your knees in the air and feet planted firmly on the sides of his torso. In this arrangement, you have complete control of the depth of penetration. You can take as little or as much as you desire.

At this stage, he can slide his body around and let his feet fall on the floor while you once again wrap your legs around his torso. Now, provided he's strong enough, he can stand up with you fully attached, encircling his torso with your arms wrapped around his neck and your legs around his waist. His arms and hands can hold your buttocks as he massages them and rhythmically pulls you on and off his protrusion.

At this time, he can walk over to a chair and sit down in it with you still fastened to his body. For a terrific feeling, you can use the base of the chair to balance and control your movements. Sitting on him, sitting in a chair is a very pleasurable and erotic sensation for both of you. A good orgasm can come from this technique.

DOGGY STYLE

In the film *Clan of the Cave Bear*, Daryl Hannah was endlessly on all fours servicing her husband. Hopefully her character was being fulfilled, too! The eroticism of penetrating from behind can be an enormous turn-on for both lovers. It's a virile thing and exceedingly primal, and some women can only achieve orgasm in this position. It blows their mind every time.

This preferred position gives your man better access to your G-spot (which is about the size of a quarter and located two or three inches inside the vagina directly behind the pubic bone and clitoris at once, plus he can control your body with graceful aplomb. By the same token, you can reach your hand through your legs and massage his scrotum. Also in the doggy position, inhibitions seem to fade for both partners, which is key to orgasm.

You can alter this position by both of you lifting your torsos together. Okay, both of you are on your knees—upright—with your back to his torso. His advantage is that he can kiss your turned face, massage your breasts and clitoris while sliding in and out at a desired angle. At this point, he can sit back on his heels while you sit back, resting on him.

With a little more energy and still connected, he can lie back on his elbows while you sit on his erection with your legs over his knees and possibly wrapped around his torso. From this very sexy position, he sits up as you bend over, placing your elbows on the floor for support and resting your head on your forearms. Of course your legs are wrapped around his waist backwards, right? Your genitalia is facing his face. His penetration is seriously erotic and visual. He can see, play, and satisfy as he takes over the floor.

Next! Still connected, but with the same flowing rhythm, he's lying down again as you stretch your left leg out and over his left shoulder. His left leg is bent and to the side of your left torso. His right leg is curved over your right extended leg. In this position, you are almost completely on your stomach and he is completely on his back. He has better control of penetration, but your wild tigress can still roar.

This would be a good time to disconnect for a while and in the same position, slide your genitals back gently into his mouth as you position your mouth on his fields of Bali.

POSTERIOR SLIDE-IN

You can lie on your stomach while your man approaches your vagina from behind, laying his chest on your back. You can enjoy the weight of his pelvis hitting your buttocks and the length of his penis traveling between your legs, arriving at your vagina. For more rhythmic waves, he can put a pillow under your buttocks and satisfy that G-spot a bit more.

CUDDLE POSITION

This is nice for waking up in the morning. You're both on your sides facing in the same direction (often called "making spoons"). He slips his penis into your vagina from the back. He can also hold your slightly bent leg up as he slides his penis and his legs in between yours. The advantage is the snug, cozy, comfortable fit as well as the ability to massage your breasts and clitoris and hug you from behind. It's a very loving position.

WORKERS' POSITION

It's a variation of the cuddle. You roll onto your back while he stays on his side. You lift your leg closest to him and place it over his pelvis to give his penis access to your vagina. For the sake of comfort, he inserts his top leg between your legs. From this position he can easily suck on the breast closest to his mouth. This position is for lovers who are a bit tired from long hours of work.

Any position is great, as long as it's comfortable for both lovers. The way your bodies fit together will determine the best sequence for any given position. It's amazing how creative lovers become after experimenting a few times. Invent. Use your instincts. Go with the flow. Flash and dash with maximum confidence.

A few tips: Work with his penis to find what rhythms and pressures he enjoys the most. Also experiment with angles that will give you good hip mobility. In this way, you can control the rhythm and tempo of the complete sex act. Use your hips and pelvic area to pump and slide—up and down, around and around, side to side, as your vaginal muscles squeeze and release, squeeze and release.

As you maintain a graceful rhythmic flow, your tempo will vary in degrees. The spiral growth of your vine tendrils should start to wrap around his penis and pull him in slowly while you gently open wider—inch by delicious inch—feeling his firm tenderness inside your warm, wet enticement.

After a great while, when you sense the time is right, accelerate from a slow leisurely walk of holding hands, smelling the flowers, and getting to know him, to a moderate trot. Only when you feel absolutely primed, harmoniously ride into a quickened pace—fast, faster, fastest. At which point, he is probably beginning to end. Ahhh, such immense vibrations to his penis!

Also, know that when your lover first penetrates, he will automatically begin to gauge the depth of your vagina. It's his natural instinct. His penis is measuring how much depth he has to play with—whether you have a shallow or deep vaginal vault. This lets him know what action to take, how to react to your enthusiastic aggressions, and when to go forward. That's essential for a duet. Allow him to survey the exact width and circumference of your vault. In case it's shallow, he may accidentally push too hard, too soon, and bang up against your cervix, sending you screaming in pain. It's a good idea always to take him in slowly before playtime.

In a luscious and loving moment, take him in completely and let him rest inside your walls while the only movement between the two of you is your vaginal muscles squeezing and releasing, hugging, gripping, massaging, and playing with his organ. It's a great sensation for a fella to just hang out while your muscles make magic around his wand. But please understand that your progressive movements may feel too good and he may ask you to stop moving for fear of losing his cool. A perfect example is the intimate lovemaking scene between Robert Redford and Meryl Streep in the film *Out of Africa.* Redford whispers to Streep, "Don't move!" She says, "But I want to move!" He repeats with complete conviction, "Don't move!!" The translation is: "You feel so good, I'm ready to explode. If you move a muscle, I'll come right now." The choice is yours. If you want the lovemaking to end . . . move. If you want it to continue . . . do as he asks.

Now, when you hear those beautiful words from the breath of your lover, your heart will silently smile. I admit, it is tempting to feel the meat of the matter at that sexy, vulnerable moment, but providing you want more, I suggest you allow him a few seconds to compose himself before you restart your engine. The words *don't move* are his way of saying, "Honey, you're incredible, I'm losing control!" N-I-C-E . . .

Take this opportunity to compliment his sexiness —his manliness. Seductive sounds can be highly effective. Keep your words truthful and simple: "Your hair smells so good, your hands are so strong, your skin is beautiful, you make me so wet, I want your tongue everywhere. I want to feel all of you." Then when you're ready for him to ejaculate you can say, "Come inside of me. Come deep inside of me. Deeper, deeper, harder. Yes, Oohh, yes. Yes, yes, *yessss*!!" My feeling is that you will probably both orgasm together. But let's enhance his pleasure a bit longer before you do. Remember, *you* are driving the car! Go where you wanna go.

Anyway, I know I refer to the sac that holds his two perfectly cut diamonds quite a lot, but try not to forget them. While holding his jewels securely in your hand, think of being in Tiffany's and having the gems between your fingers, feeling all the facets—the brilliance, the fascination. With the same sentiment, gently work his testes in a circular motion. Feel them rolling in their sac. It's a kind of loving sensation for both of you.

Again, pay attention to his every nuance. He will quietly or silently let you know what pressure he prefers—gentle, more firm, or none at all. Follow his lead and give him what he wants. As he penetrates in and out, find a rhythm of massaging his testicles that coincides with the rhythm of his motion. Also, gently slide your finger up and down his perineum—the area between his anus and scrotum. Your fingers will intoxicate him. It's also extremely sexy to circle your thumb and forefinger around the base of his shaft as he's sliding in and out of your vagina. A little pressure can be enjoyable; however, too much of a good thing can cause the cake to bake prematurely! And we don't want that to happen just yet, do we, ladies?

Licking, sucking, and touching his neck, shoulders, mouth, nipples, ears, and fingers are erotic during intercourse. Don't stop your heavenly touches because "foreplay" has ended and "intercourse" has begun. All of your parts should continue to be giving him pleasure. And don't use the same tactile stimulation pattern for too long. It gets boring. Stimulation should be exhilarating.

I talked about the frenulum of his penis being one of his G-spots. Well, his other G-spot is his prostate. You may want to explore this sensation; you may not. If you decide to touch upon it, clean, clean, clean is key. Some men will invite your explorations, while others may feel embarrassed, awkward, and violated. I'm sure he'll let you know immediately exactly what his feelings are on the subject, either verbally or with silent and very tight body contractions. Like, "*No!* Not there! Don't touch *that*!"

Unfortunately, to touch his prostate you must go through the rectum. That's the rub. To make matters more difficult, the anal area does not produce its own lubricant. There is also an element of "total recall." Many men associate this sort of probing to the extreme discomfort of a similar procedure given during their physical examinations at the doctor's office. It happens to be a crucial part of his physique. No wonder a man gets nervous. Wouldn't you?

Yet there are many uninhibited men who may encourage your gentle rummaging. If so, make sure you have plenty of lubrication at your disposal. Make sure your nails are short and smooth and that you enter gently and slowly with great sensitivity, as though it were your own private part.

His prostate is located a few inches inside the rectum on the anterior (front) wall. It's about the size and shape of a walnut. Proper massage of the area is actually a healthy deterrent to future prostate problems. I'm not recommending that you do this, but when he's ready to orgasm, a little prostate massage will detonate the dynamite.

Did you know that a lot of people around the world engage in touching and probing of the anus but refuse to talk about it? Some men insert finger size vibrators for added stimulation. The anus is all part of your anatomy, like your mouth. In fact, it's the bottom of your throat, isn't it? It's important to always keep it clean with thorough washing and proper diet.

After you've discovered the opulent and naughty treasures at the bottom of his emerald sea with your inviting glance, touch, movements, enhance his pleasure by expressing your true erotic needs and feelings. For example: "Wait, slower, yes, that's it, faster, harder, no, not yet, hmmmmmmm . . . hold it, yes, ohhh, that feels so good, yes, stay—just stay there. Oh, I like that . . . it feels so good. Ohh, don't move, let me grab onto you, let me feel you. I love your thickness. Yes, that's right, slow and easy. Give me more. I want to feel more of you—deeper, deeper, yes . . . give me more, more, more. Oh yes, that's it. Faster, faster, deeper. I feel you growing inside me. It's so big and hard!" Express all of your emotions. Verbalize. It will only serve to heighten his ecstasy.

When you have arrived at this final destination and you know that he's throbbing to release, if you're also ready to experience the highest form of orgasm—that sacred ground of the universe where you melt and mold into one being, catch his rhythm, and ride his wave into the vibrant orange, yellow, red, and amber hues of the sunset—tell him, "Come with me, come now, please come. I want you to fill my body with your hot come. Yes, yes, *yes*, *yessssssss*!!!"

As you feel his semen flooding your insides, suck gently on his tongue in the same rhythm as his penis is pulsating inside your womb. Talk about otherworldly? Hmm, ummm! Your vaginal muscles will organically pulsate around his penis as you both contract in orgasmic delirium.

During this dizzying orgasm, you will not know where he ends and you begin. It's the ultimate symbolism of sexuality and true love. Your mind leaves you. Your twitching, quivering body and soul belong to him; and his blushing heap of muscle, sinew, and significance belongs to you. The two of you truly become god and goddess in the empyreal land of Zeus. You don't exist anymore. He doesn't exist. Your wet, sublime molecular structures are swimming in the ocean of embryonic fluids united in poetic motion.

For variety, he may want to be nasty and come on your breasts, your stomach, your back, your face, or in your mouth. If that's his choice and yours, let him pull out and enjoy. It can be very exciting for him to watch while his semen expresses itself all over your body or inside whatever orifice he chooses to implement. You have no idea how exciting love play can be for the two of you until you let go—explore, experiment, and invent.

Before we leave this section, I want to inject a warning. If you're on top of your gent and you accidentally bend yourself backward, it's extremely possible to hurt the spongelike tissue inside his organ. Also, torsion, which is a twisting of the testicles, can obstruct the penis's blood supply and kill off the testicles. Please be careful. His organs are much more delicate than you can imagine.

If you use a reasonable amount of care combined with a little skill, a little practice, a lot of imagination and love, you can make intercourse a glorious experience each and every time.

A WOMAN'S PLEASURE

One half of the world cannot understand the pleasures of the other.

—JANE AUSTEN

I've given you some techniques for pleasing men. These techniques are, after all, essential elements of a seductress's tool kit. But never underestimate the importance of finding your own pleasure—not only for your sake, but also for his. A woman who is responsive and enjoys the act of making love is a much more exciting partner than one who is diligently working away, practicing her technique, but deriving no pleasure or joy from the act herself. I promise you, men can tell the difference. If you don't naturally explode in pleasure, you can learn how. And after you've learned it, you can show your man when you're in bed together.

Imagine that you're the legendary Sacagawea guiding your Lewis or Clark on the expedition of his life. Lewis and Clark might have received the credit, but it was Sacagawea's instinct, knowledge, bravery, and guidance that paved the way. However, if Sacagawea had not known the territory, the expedition would have been a tragic failure. You can't travel up that mountain unless you know exactly what your body and spirit needs for the ultimate journey. So first become a connoisseur of your own body. Explore it to discover what areas give you pleasure when touched and what kind of touching or stroking is most effective. When you know what touch, pressure, and stimulation genuinely feel good to you, you can communicate that information to your man. Show him by touching him in the ways you would like to be touched and say the words out loud. Men like to hear them.

It's a biological fact of life that men don't have to spend a lot of time positioning themselves, being in the "right mood," or feeling sexy to enjoy a good release —ejaculation feels good whenever it happens. We women do need to be in the right mood and feel sexy. But don't make the mistake of thinking you are at the mercy of your mood as if it were some kind of weather over which you have no control. You can make choices to adjust and manipulate your mood.

One way to get into a sexy mood is the use of

imagery. Think: I am beautiful, I am wonderful, I am special, I love my hands, my breasts, my legs, my hair, my womanhood. Another way is to treat your physical senses. Turn off the world and turn on your favorite music. Run a warm, soothing, bubbly tub; light a few candles; use gels, oils, or slippery soaps to spread all over your entire body. Now you're stimulating the senses of hearing, sight, smell, and touch. This is a good time to explore your body. Feel your softness and cherish your lotus blossom. Before you leave the tub, use a handheld shower or open your legs and let the faucet water run over your clitoris, but make sure the water is comfortable for your delicate parts. You may orgasm, but if not, continue to rub oils or lotions on your soft clean skin, paying more attention to your nipples and clitoris. Is this helping to put you in a sexy mood? If it isn't, try something else.

Some women get into a sexy mood by wearing certain kinds of clothing. But it's different kinds of clothing for different women. For some, it's silky lingerie. For others it's beautifully cut classic clothes in wonderful fabrics. Other women feel very sexy when they're wearing tight jeans, leather, latex, or Lycra, and others feel beautiful in gowns of billowing silk, chiffon, or lace. Find out which outfits make you feel like the "It" Girl. No one but you has to know why you're wearing them. But the sexy mood you're feeling will give off positive vibrations.

Put on an erotic video, read sexy passages from a book or magazine, and look at erotic pictures of other women, men, or couples. Buy erotic toys—whatever excites your libido. Just do it! Do whatever you deem necessary to promote pleasure.

Drink wine or champagne if it helps you feel more free. Guide your lover's hands up and down the length of your body, exploring all erotic portals. Learn which

parts are hungry for attention. When you find them
. . . experiment. What touch turns you on? What type
of stroke do you prefer—long or short? What kind of
pressure do you enjoy—light or firm? What type of
rhythm feels best—fast or slow?

Let's move on . . . Teaching your man to give you
the proper stimulation to orgasm during cunnilingus is
extremely difficult. Either he has a mobile tongue and
loves a woman's juicy vagina or he doesn't. Learning
fellatio is much easier for you than it is for him to learn
how to properly give you cunnilingus. He needs to have
an aptitude and a strong desire with no hang-ups.

You must be exceedingly clean for him to draw
pleasure from the experience. The only way to really
show him is to literally let him put his face between
your legs as you massage and titillate your own femininity. Now let him watch as you pleasure your love
bud. Then encourage his fingers to mimic your previous
motions by either placing your fingers over his and
guiding him or slowly whispering your needs. Men
learn very fast when they're given specific instruction.
They understand clarity.

So as he licks, don't be shy in letting him know
what strokes, pressures, tongue rhythms, fingers or no
fingers, you prefer. Again, relaxation and rhythm are
everything. Without the proper rhythm you won't orgasm during intercourse or cunnilingus. This, of course,
takes practice and plenty of patience.

Remember the old joke where the stranger in New
York asks a passerby how to get to Carnegie Hall? The
answer was "Practice, practice, practice." That's what's
needed here. But in this instance, the practice itself can
be a lot of fun. And when the desired level of expertise
is achieved, each of you will be playing in a throbbing,
pulsing duet.

HOW TO MASTURBATE

One of the most effective ways to learn how to pleasure your own body is to masturbate. Does the subject embarrass you? It shouldn't. "Hey, don't knock masturbation! It's sex with someone I love" (from the film *Annie Hall*).

To be a goddess, a magnificent seductress, you need to feel, understand, and express all of your womanhood. You must experience orgasm. God gave you all the tools, all the parts. Work with them, use them for your pleasure, and the pleasure of your lover, your main man.

Alan Jay Lerner reminds us that "Pleasure without joy is as hollow as passion without tenderness." The word *pleasure* comes from the Old French *plaisir*, which means "to please." Before you can please anyone, you must first rid yourself of that block in your brain that tells you pleasure is not good. Pleasure *is* good!!! Pleasure is what every female needs to feel and express to be complete. You deserve all the joy and sensual gratification in life—simply because you're you.

Relax. Open your mind, and feel your sensuality. Give yourself a present wrapped in joy with a card attached that reads: To Yourself . . . From Yourself.

No one can awaken your sensuality as well as you. Only you hold the key that unlocks the door to Wonderland. Your brain is the lock, your fingers are the key. You are on your own. Are you ready, Alice?

Prepare to love yourself for at least thirty minutes or more in total seclusion. Find a part of the house—basement, attic, garage, or separate room—where you can lie down in a soft comfortable spot. Make certain that you will not be disturbed, and if possible, put on slow, sensual music, turn the lights low or light a candle, burn incense or spray the room with your perfume, drink a few sips of wine or champagne, and wrap your body in a silky piece of lingerie. Actually, a warm room is preferable, but if you don't have immediate access to these accoutrements, work with what you've got at hand—you and your imagination. That's all you need anyway.

Now lie down. Take your time to explore. Go very slowly—very, very slowly. Start touching the fabric of your gown over your skin. Touch your hair, your ears, your nose, your lips, your throat. Slide your fingers up and down your arms and shoulders, pass over your breasts, touching your stomach, your navel, your hips, and down your thighs. Feel the warmth of your silky skin emanating through the fabric. Stroke your thighs on the outside, then slightly part your legs and run your fingers along their inner flesh. Feel the texture, the smoothness of your skin. Feel the warmth of your hands traveling back up your body, reaching the softness of your breasts. Circle your hand all around the plumpness of your breasts, brushing over your nipples. Gently slide the fabric over their erectness. Observe their color and shape. Pinch them, make them harder. Lick your index finger and circle it around the protrusion of the nipple. Roll it slightly between your thumb and index finger. Squeeze it. Play with it for a while. Enjoy the sensation. Now use both hands to massage your breasts. Feel your sensitive nipples as you massage. As you gently squeeze and pull them, you can also feel throbbing sensations arising from your clitoris. You are experiencing their direct line of communication.

Now take a few deep breaths and let your hands drift down your navel and over your thighs again. Ever so gently, lift the cloth up as you feel that triangle of curly hair between your thighs. Look at the beauty of your erect nipples as you caress the outside of your nether lips. With your fingertips, tug slightly on your curly hairs. Feel how they are connected to your ripening vulva. Run your finger up and down the smoothness of your silky inner lips. Open your legs wider. Slide your index finger down the hot, moist crevice, feeling the desire of your beautiful and natural secretions. See how your body is responding to your touch? It's moaning in silence.

Put the same moist finger up to your parted lips. Lick it with your tongue. Taste and smell your own sweet nectar. Now liberally wet your fingers and put them back on your aroused clitoris (the highly sensitive knob that protrudes slightly just underneath the pubic bone). With your probing fingers, very gently move the hood up and down to stimulate arousal. Try to focus more on your left side. Because there are more nerve endings on that side, sensations tend to be greater. Experiment with different rhythms, different pressures, until you find the desired touch for your particular pleasures.

As you play, always be gentle. Since your rosebud is the most sensitive part of your genitalia, it does not like direct stimulation. So take care not to hurt it. With a little tenderness, it will reward you greatly. (And beware of too much intense stimulation. This could result in numbness of the area, thereby ruining your orgasm.) With the proper stimulation, your entire feminine area will become more and more sensitive with its increasing engorgement. You are on your way to the joy of complete pleasure.

Gently reduce the pressure, but continue the natural rhythm you have found. Continue to relax, to breathe, to enjoy this delicious moment. Your face will be flush, your nipples will be hard, your heart will be racing. At this point, you have found the right plateau. (If you haven't, a little troubleshooting may be in order. Try adjusting pressure and rhythm until you find the right balance.) Your body will easily remember these sensations; they are like a guidepost for future sessions. Do not try to orgasm just yet, continue to ride the wave.

Orgasm at this stage is not important. What is important is that you find a comfortable and stimulating rhythm and pressure. When you hit the right plateau, the force of life will take over. Orgasm generally follows when you let your body take over your mind. However, don't make the mistake of stopping once you feel it coming on. This is not the end. The end occurs when you feel several contractions in a row. In a word, keep stimulating until you can stimulate no more—until it becomes too sensitive to touch. Then you know you've done it. Alice has been to Wonderland.

P.S. Don't forget to breathe and do not masturbate to excess. Once or twice a day is okay—from time to time, but too much will desensitize you, rub the hairs of your pubis away, and diminish the possibility of intense orgasm with your man.

Masturbation is not only the most useful and widely used substitute for loving sex with a partner, but it is also the way to taking your lovemaking to new heights by increasing your awareness of your own body.

FOR THE EXPERIENCED

For you ladies who are experienced at masturbation, you may want to try something new and fun. Since you already know your body, maybe this creation will offer a little more satisfaction, titillation, or extended lustiness.

Always make sure that you are undisturbed for at least an hour. Lie down on your bed, couch, or floor in front of a mirror, if you will. Bring yourself to that euphoric feeling by massaging the hood of your clitoris with your wet fingers. As the erotic sensations increase, slip several fingers of the other hand into your vagina, hook them upward and massage your G-spot (urethral sponge) at your heartbeat rate. As your vagina expands, add more fingers, keeping it half full. When you feel the need to orgasm, resist the sensation. Stay relaxed and keep that lovin' feeling. The sensation will increase, and by resisting orgasm at this point, you will feel simultaneous pleasure/pain.

Now your right hand is pushing against the clitoral hood while the fingers of your left hand are feeling the spongy tissue inside while pushing against your G-spot (which is really the back of the clitoris). Now you are performing a "bimanual palpation" of the clitoris. This heartbeat rhythm actually pinches the clitoris, urging on a swell of jubilation. You can feel your walls twitching at your heartbeat rate. But don't be fooled. It's not an orgasmic contraction . . . just a twitch!

P.P.S. Some women use vibrators to enhance this method. If you become too attached to your vibrator, you might become impatient with your main man. And that would be a shame.

At this time, you will arrive at the spiritual level . . . When orgasm starts, stop all stimulation! More stimulation at this point will probably be painful. Your vagina should powerfully contract about six times, then pause for one contraction. Squeeze your PC muscles and stroke your love bud a few more times. The orgasm should increase and your vagina will go another six contractions. Your entire body will feel like one big clitoral head in a whole-body orgasm.

During this whole-body orgasm, you are already self-excited, so do not apply any hand stimulation. Nevertheless, leave your hands in place. Especially, leave your fingers in your vagina. It needs something to squeeze and push against to continue orgasm; otherwise it stops. Oftentimes, by applying a steady pressure on the hood of your clitoris with your outer hand, it can increase your orgasmic sensations.

At contraction twelve, there will be another pause. Squeeze your PC muscles, give your clitoris a few more strokes, and you will fly out of your body. Time and place and space will escape reality. Your feminine senses will be swimming in the high seas of erotic sexuality. You may hear the romantic voice of Luis Miguel accompanied by the classical guitar of Segovia serenading your orgasms in the distance.

Utopia will be reached, ideally, when you teach your man to take you to this place. After this experience, he will never leave you and you will never leave him. Not after crossing over into the divine milieu—the realm of spiritual eroticism—together!

MASTURBATION

Love is like cigarette smoking. If you smoke four or five a day you enjoy the smoke to the fullest. If you smoke two packs, you get nothing out of it but hardening of the arteries.

—HENRY MILLER

"It's pink. It's hard like an engorged weeping animal— a live piece of flesh—a succulent plant growing out of the moss of pubic hair engorged with fluid. The open slit which looks like a little mouth is waiting to kiss or be kissed. Then the mouth gets full and ejaculates," says Graham, a thirty-nine-year-old journalist in Washington, D.C.

From a man's point of view, this definitely explains why masturbation makes a fella feel alive and well. It's a way of loving himself, so to speak. We all know that love is blind, so a man needs to feel his way around!

Of course, there are many other reasons a man engages in this visual heaven: he enjoys watching his symphony grow and feeling its thin, sensitive skin; reveling in the nerve sensations while it fills with blood and stiffens; experiencing lewd fantasies during its awakening; and hearing Ludwig van Beethoven's "Ode to Joy" from his Ninth Symphony, while seeing bright lights and angels at the finale.

His penis is naturally on the outside of his body, so he can watch fluids flow from the little slit at its head while he's massaging it, then spreading the slippery secretion around the shaft.

The delicious sensation of masturbation also allows a man to forget his worldly woes for a few stolen moments. He wanders into his testosterone head where only warriors can see the other side. Because no matter how strong a woman's orgasm or how rejuvenated, enthusiastic, and relaxed she feels, it will never produce the same effect that a man experiences when he ejaculates. It is magic to him. When he's done, he can even go outside and give a thirsty branch or tree a golden shower from several feet before it lands. It's a lot of fun for a man to put his hands on all that miraculous equipment and watch its workings. When it's working and giving him pleasure, it makes him feel proud and thankful that he is a man.

Men who especially love the missionary position have been known to use pillows (the soft, downy kind) for masturbation. For example, when men masturbate, not only is it common practice to use their hand with a bit of lubrication spread over the penis, but certain men have discovered a way to actually duplicate the feeling of the woman they fantasize. For example, while in the missionary position the man puts on a condom, faces downward on the bed, places a pillow underneath his stomach with his testicles free-falling, and another pillow underneath his chest. He circles his arms around the latter as if he were hugging the woman, then proceeds into a copulating motion. I'm told it's a great facsimile. You would be surprised to learn just how many men continue to masturbate after marriage. A lot! Mary Louise, twenty-six, has been married to Glen, thirty-four, for eight months. One morning, she returned home after forgetting her briefcase to find Glen still in bed holding a pornographic magazine in one hand while the other hand was massaging his member. She was taken aback at the sight.

Mary Louise could not believe her eyes. She and Glen had a great sex life. So why, she asked herself? Before Mary Louise married Glen, she knew that he was prone to compulsive masturbation, but she believed that marriage would change him. Wrong! Marriage doesn't change anyone. Instead, the comfort of marriage brings out the real person. If a man derives joy in self-stimulation, oftentimes he will continue. Married men *do* masturbate! It's not bad or abnormal. Wouldn't you rather he masturbate than have coitus with another woman? Think about it!

When a man masturbates, there's a lot more going on than just the physical activity; his *imagination* is creating sexual fantasies in glorious living Technicolor and stereophonic sound that is akin to virtual reality. Try to get your man to share his fantasies with you. Knowing exactly what arouses his imagination is advantageous to your lovemaking.

During my interviews, a lot of men were embarrassed to reveal that intimate part of themselves for fear of being judged improperly. However, a few strangers did express themselves rather enthusiastically. They all came from a different background of fantasies. For instance: Ross, thirty-two, a paralegal in Saint Louis, Missouri, and married, said: "I was obsessed with these three girls in my office. They all looked different—different color hair, faces, bodies, but all tens. For weeks I couldn't talk to them without seeing them naked in my imagination. Driving home I would fantasize all three of them in my cubicle at work. They would all be completely naked except for wearing CFMs (come-fuck-me four-inch spike heels). One would be sitting on my desk with her legs spread-eagle, playing with herself. The second girl would be sitting in my chair, sucking on her nipples and bouncing her tits, and the third would be standing in the conference room door, waiting to undress me when I arrived. They were there to give me pleasure.

"The girl standing in the door unzipped my pants and sucked my cock. The girl sitting in my chair walked over and while putting her tits in my mouth said, 'Suck on these, big boy!' The girl sitting on my desk turned around and got on all fours with her pussy facing me while she masturbated herself to orgasm. They were all down and talkin' dirty. I loved it! I know it was unrealistic, but it's that unrealistic quality that turns me on."

Does Ross's wife have anything to worry about regarding these three co-workers? Probably not. But she might feel a little intimidated, to say the least. This is a situation where Ross's discriminating good judgment should take over. Certain fantasies might be harmful to the relationship if vocalized unless a woman is completely self-confident and not the jealous type. Do you know any?

The dominating power of a woman can inspire many a male fantasy. Darrin, thirty-seven, a stamp collector living in Sioux City, Iowa, relates an ongoing fantasy that most men have about attractive lady doctors. "I was on my way to a dental appointment. I hate going to the dentist. I usually put off my appointment until the pain is so excruciating, I have no choice. One day, it was an emergency. My appointment was the last one of the day. To my surprise, my usual dentist had taken ill and a stunning woman, Dr. Taylor, filled in.

"I sat down in the chair. Dr. Taylor started probing around in my mouth, trying to find the root of the problem. She found it, shot me with Novocain, and it started: As she cradled my head in her arms, her breast softly brushed against my face. She said, 'Open wide! Yeah, that's right. Stay just like that. Move your tongue over to the side. Now, keep it there. Open a little more. Good, good, don't move, stay where you are. Yeah, that's it!'

"She dabbed the side of my mouth with a napkin. All of a sudden, my fears diminished. All I could think about was having her. I shut my eyes and felt her fingers slowly unzipping my trousers. She rubbed and massaged my penis before she slid her hand inside. Her hand knew exactly what I wanted. I felt like exploding. Before I realized it, she was straddling the chair and me. She unbuttoned her blouse and opened her bra, exposing pink nipples. She decisively leaned over, unhooked the nitrous oxide and placed it over my face. Then she inhaled a bit herself as she sat on my erection. She put my hands on her breast and held onto them as she massaged them back and forth. Her hips were gyrating. Her pussy was sucking me to orgasmic spasms.

"You wanted to know my fantasy? Now you know. That was an ongoing picture reeling around in my mind every time I saw my lady dentist. Unfortunately, Dr. Taylor moved. Now I have a male dentist. Nope, I've got nothin' to add to that!"

Some men are into pain-dominance from a mistress figure. Others like Al, twenty-eight, a gofer on a movie set in Madison County, Virginia, enjoy fantasy subservience. Al confides, "When I masturbate, I like to think of my girlfriend wearing a mask, thigh-high black leather boots with spike heels, a black bra with the nipples cut out, and crotchless black panties. She's my mistress and I'm her slave boy. She ties my hands behind my back. She walks over to me with a dominating look in her eyes, slapping a paddle against her leg. She commands me to get down on my knees and lick her boots and then she puts her spike heel into my mouth and says 'Suck.' When I do something that displeases her she thrashes my bottom with the paddle. She orders me to lick and suck her entire body. She makes me stay there until she is completely appeased. When I don't please her, she pushes my mouth away and makes me wait while she does it herself to show me the proper way. Then she makes me do it over and over until I get it right." If Al's girlfriend knew about his fantasy, she might be able to play the role and make it fun for the both of them. I wonder if Al will ever tell her.

A man's fertile mind can turn any co-worker into a sudden siren as Brendan, forty, an actor in Los Angeles, shows. He enjoys a recurring fantasy about his present leading lady. "When I return to my hotel room, usually late at night, I'm too wired to sleep. I often picture Natalie walking into my room dressed in a trench coat and high heels. She takes off the coat and underneath, her shapely, long sinuous legs are sheathed in black nylons with the narrow tabs of a black garter belt, bustier, and tons of white pearls. I watch as she unknots her raven hair, letting it cascade to her waist. She says, 'Don't touch me. Don't even move. I want you to lie still while I grind my luscious juices over your big hard rock and straddle your face!'" I wonder if Natalie knows about Brendan's feelings for her. Should he tell her? Faint heart never won fair lady.

Other men derive even greater pleasure from

slightly pain-giving fantasies where he takes on a more sadistic point of view as Jason, forty-six, an advertising executive in Savannah, Georgia, exhibits. He fantasizes himself a plantation owner giving discipline to one of his gorgeous slave girls. Once a week, he needs to show his authority: "My butler brings Sophie into my study. She grins defiantly as she walks through the door. I tell her that I will not tolerate her disobedience one more time. I pull her by her golden mane over toward the piano, where I bend her over the bench and tie her arms and legs. I go in back of her and slowly lift her skirt, the layers of petticoats exposing her bare white buttocks. I remove my belt, feeling the smooth hard leather across my palm. Then I slide it across her bare flesh and between her alabaster thighs. She squirms against her will. I stand back and lay one across her backside, watching her buttocks redden. The more they redden, the more excited I become. Watching them lift and fall, lift and fall with every swat. Her moans and groans make me delirious. After a few more licks, I stick my boot between her legs and part them even farther. I pinch her pubic lips to feel her moisture. I can see the glistening of sweet nectar flowing down her thighs. I tell her she's a bad girl and she's disappointing. I can feel my rod getting the best of me. Her writhing makes me hotter. She says, 'I'll do as you say, anything, anything, my lord, my master!' With that plea, I kneel down behind her, taking her ripe globes into my hands and opening her wider. I watch her pink folds quiver with desire. I know she's ready. I spank her with my hand once more before running my fingers up and down her lips, parting them farther. I play with her clitoris before inserting my two fingers, then three, pumping them into her pussy as she grabs onto them with her whole sex. The more she begs, the more time I take. My tongue finds her pink bud and flicks around its firmness. Then sucking, pulling, biting until I feel her body jerking from orgasm. My erection is painful. I walk in front of her, unzipping my pants to relieve my throbbing member. I hold it in my hand watching it quiver in front of her flushed and delirious face. She opens her insatiable mouth and drinks from my tumid fountain as I shove it into the depths of her throat!" This is a pretty popular fantasy, although Jason articulates it better than most men.

There are women out there who would love to role play in a bondage/domination fantasy. Maybe Jason should spend a little bit of time seeking someone out. Or, maybe, he could carefully introduce his girlfriend to the idea in easy stages. What do you think?

A lot of men watch porno flicks. It's extremely common. In their minds, they place themselves on the screen. Especially in these days of virtual reality, some men even go so far as to imagine the actress from the film they are viewing walking out of the television set and into their room. One such man is Fisher, a twenty-nine-year-old automobile assembler from Dayton, Ohio. Fisher explained to me one of his favorite fantasies, which revolved around a specific movie.

In the story, a full-figured, succulent blond woman, dressed in a black crotchless cat suit with a patch over one eye, crawls on all fours into a room where two studs are standing at each corner of a mat, stroking their erect penises. She crawls over to one guy, rises up to her knees, and begins kissing his balls and licking the shaft of his penis. She becomes ecstatic as her quivering hands and tongue wrap around his organ. The second man becomes impatient and suddenly walks over, pulls her hair back, positioning her face in front of his hard member and thrusting it in her mouth. She begins to perform the same subservient licking and sucking along his grand erection. While she's enjoying the action, the first man spreads her legs wide apart, and as he lifts her hips high in the air, pierces her from behind. With his entry, she lets out a primal cry of pleasure, and for several minutes she has multiple orgasms. After a while, both men simultaneously ejaculate—one in her mouth and the other in her vagina. They pull out and leave the mat.

Still on all fours, the blond bombshell turns around and looks straight through the TV at Fisher lying on the bed. She slowly stands up, walks through the screen into Fisher's bedroom, and proceeds to plant a wet kiss on his hungry lips, whispering, "You're next, Big Boy." Her tongue slides slowly over his body until she reaches his throbbing erection and wraps her lips around its thickness. She urgently guides his penis into her vagina and begins to gyrate her hips and squeeze her nipples in rhythm. In a frenzy, Fisher throws her on the bed, spreads her legs, lifts her buttocks, and savagely plunges into her from behind, exploding his semen deep into her wanton walls.

The gamut of male fantasies is wide, and what I have presented is a small slice of the pie. Other fantasies include golden showers, cross-dressing, voyeurism, sex with older women, sex with coeds, watching two or more girls.

In most cases, men do not live out their fantasies. But their orgasm may be associated with some kind of fantasy that is either recurrent or changing, depending upon their whim.

Let's be honest, ladies. We all need fantasies at one time or another, and some people need more than most. So if you need a little encouragement, buy a desired porno flick acted out by the people you find sexy and attractive, put on the movie, pull down the shades, and enjoy an exciting adventure with your man.

Chapter 5

If Things Go Wrong: Troubleshooting

MENOPAUSE—HIS AND YOURS

There is nothing permanent, except change.
                                    —HERACLITUS

HIS

When I first heard of male menopause, it was from my mentor, Henry Miller. I asked him if all men go through a change of life the same as women. He assured me that indeed they do, and the effects can be just as disturbing. It's all part of the aging process—waning sexual desire, losing hair, diminishing eyesight and hearing, coming to terms with his mortality. And most men in our society are just not ready for it. The ones that slide through have great self-worth and high self-esteem. They sincerely like themselves, their jobs, and their families. For them, menopause is not a bowl of cherries either, but neither is it therapy time.

Men don't get hot flashes, genital dryness, mood changes, or other symptoms associated with women, because it's not about fertility or hormones. As men age, their hormones remain steady. There is a gradual decline in testosterone production from eighteen to ninety. Around the age of thirty-five, a man begets fewer sperm and less semen, but men free from disease and illness continue to produce testosterone, sperm, and semen until the day they die.

Their angst is more about libido and mortality. Their midlife crisis is usually between ages thirty-eight and sixty. It begins when a man's body reminds him that he is no longer young. His injuries don't heel as quickly; his sex drive slightly diminishes; and he begins to fear sexual dysfunction. You know exactly what happens when fear sets in—self-doubt, weight gain, insomnia, infidelity, unhappiness at work, increased use of alcohol, low self-worth, and low self-esteem are just a few characteristics. Also, his physique, emotions, and behavior alter. During this midlife crisis of feeling unsettled and bored, men sometimes go into therapy or trade their jobs and families for newer, younger models.

The solution: relax into maturity; gain a better understanding and acceptance of the aging process; keep a sense of humor and deal with problems as they arise; eat nourishing foods, take vitamin and mineral supplements, get plenty of exercise, and change goals. Meet each day with enthusiasm, while not letting ego stand in the way. Embrace new ways of life by being grateful for the little things. They really do mean a lot.

Be supportive of your man and boost his self-esteem. Once a man has the realization of his own self-worth, that he's still sexy and appealing, that he can still enjoy good sex, he'll start to sing again. Most men become better human beings. It's all about acceptance. Accepting a new life, a new way of being, and a new attitude.

Most men realize their true selves after forty, and oftentimes are much happier in a new career. And today, several men are having children at fifty, sixty, and seventy. Look at Clint Eastwood, Sean Connery, Warren Beatty, Norman Mailer, Kirk Douglas, Ted Turner, William Devane, John Forsythe, Leslie Nielsen, Robert Redford, Sidney Poitier, Jake La Motta, Dick Clark, and others who are doing great. In fact, some are actually better, happier, and more content. All are more successful!

YOURS

We live in a generation of women who have very high expectations about looking good well into their forties and beyond. In fact, these women don't even have an age, they have a wonderful style and flair. They're also determined to stay sexually active, lustful, and romantic through it all. Let's give a cheer for those ladies! Bravo! And, there are many men who feel as did the actor Liam Neeson when he professed, "The truth is, I've always just loved women—every shape, color, age . . . and I always gravitate toward their company." Gold stars for them!

Now, for ladies who have not been introduced to menopause, or "the change," let's get familiar. First of all, it's a crying shame that your mother, aunt, or somebody doesn't prepare a woman for the biological and physiological oddities your body will undertake. Many ladies confessed that they thought they were going crazy until they went to a doctor and were told the shocking news, "You are going through menopause—get used to it!"

It happens to every woman. No woman is immune. It isn't a disease. It's just your last menstrual flow. And some women are glad, because they hate their periods —PMS and heavy flows. Your body will go through a hormonal change. Since every woman is different, her clock will vary. Some experience it as early as their thirties, others as late as their late fifties.

Hormones play an active role all through your life. Dramatic changes occur in the brain, sex hormones, and regularity of ovulation when a woman approaches her forties. Estrogen levels can drop off over a period of fifteen years, but for most women it's a brief three- to four-year span. The development of osteoporosis (depletion of calcium stored in the bones) is directly related to estrogen loss. That's the reason women can look so much older than their years. Heart disease is another common consequence.

Ovarian exhaustion is the culprit that underlies menopause—decreased vaginal lubrication, thinning of the vaginal walls, and changes in the entire genital area encompassing the urinary tract. Lack of estrogen causes tissues, nerves, muscles, veins, and organs of the pelvic area to alter. Without hormone-replacement therapy, the likelihood of vaginal and urinary infections increases, and hernias of the uterus, bladder, or bowel may occur. Hernias can protrude or totally collapse into the vaginal walls. These are just a few of the symptoms making intercourse painful.

Several women complain of numbness in the genital area, but these changes do not necessarily alter a woman's ability to have orgasms or diminish her desire, and aging by itself does not reduce a lady's libido or her ability to enjoy good sex. In fact, some women enjoy it more. Actually, the hormone associated with desire is testosterone! The adrenal glands continue to produce testosterone, and oftentimes a woman becomes "very sexy" after menopause.

At the onset of menopause, other symptoms, such as hot flashes or night sweats, insomnia, mood changes, vaginal dryness, and loss of pubic hair as well as head hair, increase when the production of estrogen and progesterone in the ovaries tapers off.

Since all women experience this change differently, and some may need more progesterone than others, it's best to see a doctor you trust to find the right combination for your particular body. What works on one woman does not necessarily work on another.

To prevent negative changes in the genitals and urinary tract, there are other alternatives available. Estrogen and progesterone creams are widely used. The sources of these creams are the barbasco plant and soybeans. (The barbasco plant is a giant yam grown in the jungles of Mexico.) Also the use of evening primrose is recommended, and 1,500 mg of calcium a day and 1,200 mg of powdered vitamin E are beneficial. If you decide to go the natural way, consult a homeopathic physician. There's no reason for any woman to suffer. You can always find a way to better health, if you investigate and keep a positive attitude.

To really understand what it must be like for a lot of women, watch the movie *Fried Green Tomatoes*. Kathy Bates gives a wonderful comical and realistic impression of what it's like to go through a change and not have a clue about what to do. Also, if you ever feel depressed, let the following women be an inspiration to you. They have either gone through it, are going through it, or will soon: Lindsay Wagner, Sandy Duncan, Sophia Loren, Candice Bergen, Ali McGraw, Angela Lansbury, Jane Fonda, Jane Seymour, Lynda Carter, Jaclyn Smith, Lauren Hutton, Victoria Principal, Cicely Tyson. These women look great and carry on full, exciting lives no matter what their age. Most of them have families, a demanding career, and celebrity to balance. A lot can be learned from these and many more admirable ladies.

HOW TO KEEP HIM ERECT

Husbands are like fires. They go out if unattended.
—ZSA ZSA GABOR

If you have ever been the recipient of a loose noodle, I don't need to tell you how awkward it is to recover from this embarrassing moment, especially for him. Women need to have a much greater understanding of this phenomenon, because there's probably not a man alive who hasn't had that curse fall upon his "friend" at some point in his life. As in: "What are you doin', buddy? This is not the time to let me down!!!"

Women are mighty lucky that they don't have to contend with such delicate matters. And delicate is an understatement. Men go through hell on earth worrying about Hoppin' Harry's health. Keeping Harry happy is a big responsibility. No matter how much a man wishes it were in his control, it's not. I've heard so many women complain about how their men get an erection every time the wind blows or with any passing beauty. Yet when his apparatus doesn't rise, those same women become undone, responding as if it were a personal affront, and often criticizing their men irreparably. You don't ever want to do that. It's just not fair.

Often a man's momentary inabilities have nothing to do with his emotions for a woman. There could be a number of reasons for his temporary impotence: insensitivity on the woman's part, fear of rejection, self-consciousness, distraction, substance abuse, stress, illness, response to medication, a death in the family, a desperate desire to please, a muscle relaxant, or a simple headache or backache. Perhaps he just doesn't feel sexy, or maybe he's worried that you may find his penis unattractive. Men are extremely sensitive about their penises.

If you subscribe to the theory that an impotent man may be the consequence of an unknowing woman, you can help dramatically. So . . . what are you going to do if this happens to you? The secret is not to bring attention to the fact that his erection is napping. For heaven's sake, don't do that!

For most men, loss of erection is mental. If and when it happens to your man . . . *empathize*. Realize that it may be hard for him to discuss the situation with you, but that it's better for your relationship if you are able to talk about it lovingly. Reassure him by letting him know that you understand his fears, worries, and anxieties . . . that his stalled engine is not important, because you love him, not his car. Don't put pressure on him. Don't start kissing, fondling, sucking, or trying to get him excited for your own ego. That's counter-productive. He must feel that you love him, no matter what.

My friend Darla had a similar situation with her boyfriend Ted. She confided, "I met this wonderful man. Everything was too good to be true. We clicked on every level. Every time we made love it was magic. Then we decided to move in together before we got married. From that moment on, he couldn't get it up. I thought it was me. But he assured me that it was just a temporary setback.

"Weeks passed and still nothing. I became really worried about our sexual relations. Then I decided to keep him busy around the house and try to keep his mind off his deflation. I suggested he build another room. He took a course in home improvement and be-gan hammering away. I also suggested that we sleep in separate beds for a while. We hugged and snuggled and kissed from time to time, but I never let it get past a certain point.

"Months passed. The added room was almost fin-ished. Ted was so proud of his accomplishment. Then one night during a rainstorm, he brought some wood in for the fireplace while I cooked a spaghetti dinner. The smell of good food, of kindling and pine; the sound of sultry jazz; and a bottle of red wine were so relaxing. I started massaging his shoulders and neck. He gave me the most delicious kiss of my life, and ka-boom, before I knew it, I was naked on the couch and Ted's detonator was about to blast off. I was in wet heaven!"

The bottom line is don't make him feel any pres-sure. Eventually, when he believes in his heart that you don't expect him to jump through hoops or give you umpteen orgasms with a twenty-four-hour-a-day erection, he *will* produce.

Of course, problems with male sexual performance run the gamut and may be deeply rooted in physical and/or psychological origins that require professional medical aid; when a problem has become progressive and long-standing, such may be the only alternative.

But, perhaps, before deciding to bring in the white coats, you and your man may want to experiment with a few physical aids to facilitate his erection. Although surgery is definitely necessary for penile implantation, there are other varieties on the market today such as: cock rings, vacuum pumps, injections, et cetera. Injections of phentolamine, papaverine, and prostaglandin as smooth-muscle relaxants at the base of the penis are commonly used.

Rings and pumps are favored by many. After erection results from arterial blood flow into the penis, these aids prevent outflow of venous blood, temporarily enlarging the penis.

Several women mimic the process during lovemaking to a milder degree. They tightly cup their hand around the man's shaft base and testicular base. He becomes thicker as he continues pumping inside her vagina. It's a turn-on for these ladies to feel his building grow bigger and harder in structure.

The more organic devices are sparking a revival of the classical styles of the nineteenth century, which grew out of the old "bow tie theory." Building on the past, as it were, men have been using this trick for thousands of years; partly because it was simple, and partly because it was plain common sense. Take the infamous Beau Brummel, for example. He allegedly claimed that he could enlarge his organ and enhance orgasm during lovemaking by untying his perfectly formed cravat and wrapping it to strangle the base of his penis. You see, there is beauty in tradition and inspiration in history.

A well-known scientist from Los Angeles, California, has discussed with me the idea of venous engorgement temporarily enlarging the penis at great length. He explained: "I advocate what I playfully refer to as Dan's Bands." Two rubber bands can make a man a king. However, it's essential that the rubber bands fit the man's penis. Rubber band sizes 82 and 83 are most commonly used by the average penis. (They are about half an inch wide with a five- and six-inch circumference.) A man can experiment by putting a number 83 rubber band behind his testicles, encasing both penis and testicles, then placing a number 82 rubber band in front of his penis at its root. The bands should fit like a glove. If they're too tight, they will shut off the circulation and that's very bad. If they're too loose, they won't work at all.

"The rubber bands restrict outflow of blood through the penile veins. The male spongy tissue (corpus cavernosum), which is erectile tissue, fills with blood and becomes more swollen. The more blood that is retained by the spongy tissue, the more will be the swelling, and hopefully the greater the penile rigidity and orgasm.

"Now, you may think this is balderdash, but you must view the penis as a balloon that can be pumped up by the man's own blood instead of hot air."

These methods are not completely fail-safe, but they can enhance penile engorgement and sexual performance. However, I do want to stress that when a problem has grown beyond a reasonable level, couples will need professional help—therapy and/or surgery.

Even within this realm, the same basic fundamentals still apply: treat your man with empathy, consideration, patience, and lots and lots of love. It's a most delicate item indeed.

HOW TO COPE WITH
PREMATURE EJACULATION

Love him, love him, love him.

—BV

"It was so exciting! He pulled up to my bumper in his long black limousine. He entered eagerly! He was slow at first because of his large size! His moves were legendary, almost magical! And then . . . it was gone," recounts Maureen, a thirty-two-year-old receptionist at Kaiser Permanente. It had promised to be an unforgettable night. It was unforgettable, all right, but not the way she had hoped.

The big question is when should ejaculation be called "premature"? Most men reach orgasm within two minutes of starting coitus. Technically, the average guy goes from penetration to ejaculation anywhere from ten seconds to three minutes. The average woman takes about eight minutes providing she's hot, thoroughly aroused, and knows how. But who cares about technical when the mood is not set and she's just beginning to spread her legs?

Bravo for the man who thinks that he's coming too quickly when he only lasts five minutes. And super bravo for the man who can wait until his woman has her mystic moment. Time is irrelevant. It all depends on how long it takes an individual woman to become completely relaxed, thoroughly stimulated, really wet, and ready to blast off. Making "great" love has nothing to do with how long. How long is a question reserved for little children who can't wait to go out to play.

Certain men just detonate too fast period, no matter whom they're making love to. Their premature ejaculation is probably due to our evolutionary past. If a man were to have lingered around in a delectable sugar wall thinking of nothing except the end of his penis, being at his most vulnerable while sexually aroused, he would probably have been eaten by a lion or other voracious carnivore.

Anthropologists say that our physical natures have not changed much in the last one hundred thousand years or so. Fortunately, today men are adaptable. A lot of men have become so goal-oriented that the result has detrimental effects. They begin to feel anxious about either having an orgasm or giving their partner one. This, however, interferes with a man's ability to relax into a pleasurable experience. Inadvertently, men who have a problem delaying detonation are considered "quick shooters."

Several of these "quick shooters" have tried all manner of things to last longer, such as numbing their penis with topical anesthetics, taking herbs, chanting, pinching themselves during intercourse, thinking about sports, a work deadline, et cetera. But premature ejaculation is not caused by an overly sensitive penis; it's simply lack of emotional control. With your considerate and loving help, he can learn how to control his orgasm.

Luckily, there are three or more methods of postponing inevitable ejaculation. One is the stop-start method, developed by James Seman, M.D. A man can either (a) masturbate during this exercise or (b) use it during intercourse. However, I feel that masturbation will yield better results, simply because a man can practice more often with no distraction, whereas inside his partner he will definitely be distracted. How does it work? When a man feels close to the point of orgasm, he should stop and rest from five to twenty seconds or when he judges it okay to continue, then begin again. This requires repetition and practice until a man can last longer than his usual or until he feels he, not "Waldo," is controlling the show. The other method is to squeeze the head or the base of his penis momentarily to slow the onset of ejaculation.

Dr. John Whipple, a psychiatrist in Topeka, Kansas, agrees that either technique can be effective.

William Masters and Virginia Johnson developed the Penile Squeeze. It works thus: when a man feels he's ready to come, he stops and pulls out. Then reenters after he and his "friend" are composed.

Another highly effective method is controlling his orgasms by contracting the same pelvic muscles that stop his urethra from expelling its golden stream. Your fella can practice this exercise while driving in his car. All it entails is the ability to contract his penis in his pants. He can do several sets of twenty repetitions.

Many doctors that I interviewed in all fields of practice recommended the simple and more pleasurable technique of pulling down the testicles. Here's how it works: when your man is ready to explode, his testicles contract, harden, and pull close to his body. It's kinda cute to watch. Pay careful attention to this moment. When his balls rise and become firm, you know that he's getting close. Take your thumb and finger and circle it at the top of his scrotum or base of his shaft and give it a gentle jerk downward. Not too hard, because you don't want to hurt him and ruin the erotic mood. It's actually fun and exciting for you to do it, but he may want to explore the feeling himself. No matter.

Whoever does it will contribute to a longer-lasting, loving, stimulating session.

Thinking about anything other than your ravishing beauty during lovemaking may be an effective way to postpone ejaculation, but it's no way to achieve harmony and togetherness. In the event a man tries everything, but nothing seems to work, there is a pleasure enhancer called "Long Joy," developed in China, based on an ancient herbal formula, and available for purchase in the United States. It's said to increase a man's endurance possibly long enough for you to reach orgasm.

But never subscribe to Murphy's Law of whatever can go wrong will. Participating in your man's glorious "point of no return" when his pelvic muscles contract in orchestration with his Cowper's gland, seminal vesicles, and prostate to spill his spectacular seed is a breathtaking occasion. The longer you can help him last, the better the sensation. Be gentle. Be patient on a continuous basis and you are sure to be rewarded by "Murphy's" new attitude.

Another positive way to view his premature ejaculations is to consider his first ejaculation as advance troops, or "sperm cadets," with the real army following soon. The night is young—talk, play, eat, drink, smoke, massage. Enjoy each other, and I assure you his army shall return! Your calla lily will blossom again, and you can get down to the real business of spending the night together, which is more than the sum total of strict sex. This is the whole experience of love.

IMPOTENCE—REAL AND IMAGINED

A man in the house is worth two in the street.
—MAE WEST

There are exceptions to every rule, but impotence is often self-induced. It can be caused by a negative mental attitude, arising from childhood humiliation or abuse, or from the feeling of inadequacy—a smaller-than-small situation. Some men seem to be born with an inferior attitude and they can't get over it.

It's not easy for certain males to keep their priorities straight. At some point in a man's life, he will suffer from temporary impotence. This occurs in about ten percent of the adult male population. Some older men suffer from recurring impotence, which can be treated either with an injection of the drug papaverine or with an apparatus such as a penile splint or implant, or even an artificial penis.

Men who have active sex lives are the lucky ones, because they are more likely to avoid the curse of impotence during old age. For most men the saying is true, "If you don't use it you might lose it!" You see, there is a muscle at the base of the penis and muscles need exercise, just as his prostate needs to be massaged. It's not advantageous for a man to fall into an asexual mode from a lengthy abstinence.

Before you throw in the towel and visit a doctor or a clinic that specializes in this type of trauma, ask him what he feels the problem is. Communication and positive, knowing action with the right woman can often be a cure. However, there are a few age-old common explanations: anxiety about his performance, fear of intimacy, possibly the wrong woman, guilt owing to religion or self-imposed ethics, depression or stress, or the influence of alcohol and drugs. But whatever the cause, don't kid yourself. Impotency, either real or self-induced, is a problem. We are what we think, remember? So if he truly thinks he has a problem, he does have a problem. Maybe he needs a change—a change of venue—a change in his sleeping patterns, eating patterns, lovemaking patterns. Sometimes all a man needs is a familiar and responsive partner and the opportunity for lively sex. Maybe he needs to know that you really want him. Try conveying a genuine interest in his pleasure. You have nothing to lose!

Epilogue

To love someone is to invite them to grow. Being happy in a relationship means communicating your needs—in bed and out of bed. Love and great sex demand everything—courtship, surprise, playfulness, humor, thoughtfulness, forgiveness, passionate moments, exercise, massage, music, good food, aphrodisiacs, and . . . a happy face!

Start today. Be positive and adventurous. Be your fantasy—the woman you admire and revere—but stay true to yourself. The secrets of seduction? Giving and receiving, controlling and surrendering, putting your whole heart and soul into pleasuring your lover, using the magic of music, candlelight, imagination, and the feel of something silky against your naked body—with complete confidence in your seductive skills. Only then will you succeed in being the greatest lover he's ever had.

On the subject of love, the actor Gerard Depardieu said, "On a movie set, when I'm working with a beautiful woman, I may enjoy a little seductive teasing. I don't go beyond that, however; I value fidelity over flirtation. Conquest is not heroic—what's heroic is to make love last!"

I'll leave you with these two thoughts: truth comes from the heart, not the tongue. And a life lived in fear is a life half lived. Happy trails . . .

Bibliography

Abelman, Paul. *The Sensuous Mouth*. New York: Ace, 1969.

Archer, W. G., ed. *The Kama Sutra of Vatsyayana*. New York: G. P. Putnam's Sons, 1963.

Balch, James F. and Phyliss A. *Prescription for Nutritional Healing*. New York: Avery Publishing Group, 1990.

Barr, Tony. *Acting for the Camera*. Boston: Allyn and Bacon, Inc., 1982.

Bechtel, Stefan. *The Practical Encyclopedia of Sex and Health*. Emmaus, PA: Rodale Press, 1993.

Burns, Minique. "Sex Drive: A User's Guide." *Essence*, vol. 21, no. 4 (Aug. 1990), 29.

Camphausen, Rufus C. *The Encyclopedia of Erotic Wisdom*. Rochester, VT: Inner Traditions International, 1991.

Chang, Stephen T. *The Tao of Sexology: The Book of Infinite Wisdom*. San Francisco: Tao Publishing, 1986.

Chia, Mantak, and Michael Winn. *Taoist Secrets of Love: Cultivating Male Sexual Energy*. Santa Fe: Aurora Press, 1984.

Cowan, Connell, and Melvyn Kinder. *Smart Women, Foolish Choices*. New York: Clarkson N. Potter, 1985.

Davis, Ben. *Rapid Healing Foods*. West Nyack, New York: Parker Publishing Company, Inc., 1980.

Dextreit, Raymond, translated and edited by Abehsera, Michel. *Our Earth Our Cure*. Brooklyn, New York: Swan House Publishing Company, 1974.

Dunne, Lavon J. *Nutrition Almanac*. 3rd ed. New York: McGraw-Hill, 1990.

Elisofon, Eliot, and Alan Watts. *Erotic Spirituality*. New York: The Macmillan Co., 1971.

Ellis, Havelock. *Psychology of Sex*. New York: Emerson Books, Inc., 1944.

Federation of Feminist Women's Health Centers. *A New View*

of a Woman's Body. Santa Monica, CA: Feminist Health Press, 1991.

Fensterheim, Herbert, and Jean Baer. *Don't Say Yes When You Want to Say No*. New York: Dell Publishing Co., 1975.

Gawain, Shakti. *Creative Visualization*. Mill Valley, Calif.: Whatever Publishing, Inc., 1978.

Grof, Stanislav. *Beyond the Brain*. Albany: State University of New York Press, 1985.

Hartman, W., and M. Firthian. *Any Man Can*. New York: St. Martin's Press, 1984.

Hopkins, Andrea. *The Book of Courtly Love*. Harper San Francisco: Labyrinth Publishing, 1994.

Jacobsen, Karl. *Dynamic Intercourse*. New York: Cybertype Corp., 1967.

Keen, Sam. *Fire in the Belly*. New York: Bantam Books, 1991.

Kendall, Henry O., Kendall, Florence P., and Wadsworth, Gladys E. *Muscles: Testing and Function*. 2d ed. Baltimore: The Williams and Wilkins Co., 1971.

Ladas, Alice K., Whipple, Beverly, and Perry, John D. *The G-Spot*. New York: Holt, Rinehart, and Winston, 1982.

Lloyd, Joan E. *Nice Couples Do*. New York: Signet, 1959.

Ludwig, Emil. *Cleopatra—The Story of a Queen*. New York: Garden City Publishing Co., Inc., 1939.

Ludwig, Emil. *Napoleon*. New York: Garden City Publishing Co., Inc., 1926.

M. *The Sensuous Man*. New York: Dell Publishing Co., 1971.

Masters, William H., Johnson, Virginia E., and Kolodny, Robert C. *Masters and Johnson on Sex and Human Loving*. Boston: Little, Brown, 1982.

McKenna, Terence. *Food of the Gods*. New York: Bantam Books, 1992.

Milonas, Rolf. *Fantasex*. New York: Grosset & Dunlap Publishers, 1975.

Moore, George. *Héloïse and Abélard*. New York: Liveright Publishing Corporation, 1921.

Nin, Anaïs. *Aphrodisiac*. New York: Crown Publishers, 1976.

Parsons, Alexandra. *Facts & Phalluses*. New York: St. Martin's Press, 1989.

Reich, Wilhelm. *The Function of the Orgasm.* New York: Simon & Schuster, 1973.

Rector-Page, Lynda G., N.D., Ph.D. *Healthy Healing: An Alternative Healing Reference.* 9th ed. Healthy Healing Publications, 1992 and 1994.

Reinisch, June M. *The Kinsey Institute New Report on Sex.* New York: St. Martin's Press, 1990.

Rohen, Johannes W., Yokochi, Chihiro, and Romrell, Lynn. *Color Atlas of Anatomy.* New York: Igaku-Shoin Medical Publishers, 1993.

Rutgers, J. *How to Attain and Practice the Ideal Sex Life.* New York: Cadillac Publishing Co., 1940.

Shepard, Martin. *Ecstasy.* New York: Moneysworth, 1977.

Taberner, P. V. *Aphrodisiacs: The Science and the Myth.* London and Sydney: Croom Helm, 1985.

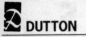